If I don't have a condom, can I use a baggie?

If I don't have a condom, can I use a baggie?

Raymond D. Fete

Moonlight Madness Publications
Massillon, Ohio

ISBN: 0-9713554-8-7

Published by:
Moonlight Madness Publications
876 Amherst N.E.
Massillon, Ohio 44646
330-833-8516

Printed by:
J&K Printing
1728 Navarre Road S.W.
Canton, Ohio 44706
330-456-5306

DEDICATION

This book is dedicated to all the parents who are willing to set the bar high for their children. Parents who know that what is popular is not always right; and what is right is not always popular. My wife is one of those parents. Thank you Wendy.

TABLE OF CONTENTS

Introduction

I have been an abstinence education presenter for nearly 20 years. I have presented my message of 'sexual abstinence until marriage' to tens of thousands of young people. I have presented to groups as small as three students and to groups as large as 3,000 students.

In every case I have enjoyed the challenge of what initially appeared to be a nearly impossible, uphill swim. Surprisingly though, I found that students were accepting, even relieved when they heard the message of abstinence until marriage. In nearly every school I have visited I have been thanked for letting young people know it is "O.K. to say no" to sexual activity.

I was not certain of how our presentation would be accepted when we first started the program. At the time I was the director of development at Mercy Medical Center, a major Catholic hospital in northeast Ohio. I was also in my 7th year as the volunteer girls basketball coach at a local Catholic elementary school. I really enjoyed the challenge of coaching 7th and 8th grade girls. Many times, their parents would drop them off for the first practice of the season, saying only "good luck!" I considered my time coaching well spent and the investment of energy a worthy one. In fact, I am still with it some 22 years later.

While in my 7th year I had the additional challenge of one of my 8th grade players facing an unplanned pregnancy. This revelation followed closely the news of several former players becoming pregnant in high school. This was especially troubling to me. I had coached these girls and I had seen the promise in them. They each had a special spark of intelligence and creativity that sadly was prevented from fully blossoming. The girls, in every case, were left holding the bag alone. The fathers had all made hasty exits from the picture. It was so troubling that I realized someone had to step up to the plate and do something to reverse this newly emerging trend.

I decided to approach my employer about the problem with the hope that, as a hospital, they might be willing to develop some specialized program to address this issue. The response was one of those "good news – bad news" situations. The good news was that the Hospital believed they should step up to provide programming to address this and other teen issues. The bad news was that they put me in charge of it.

So I quickly set about the task of assembling a committee in order to construct the best program possible. Large hospitals being what they are means that committees abound. Suffice it to say that there was not an overwhelming response to join my particular committee. Two individuals stepped forward to assist me in the task ahead. Both were not only employed there, but lived there as well. My partners in crime were Catholic nuns.

We made an interesting trio and wasted no time getting to the task at hand. We each had a list of issues we felt were important to cover in the program. We decided fairly early on to limit the number of issues in the program to four. In order to get down to a workable final four concessions had to be made. In short order we had identified four half major teen issues; alcohol use and abuse, guns and violence, sex and sexuality, and smoking. We decided to bring students from all the local Catholic elementary schools to the hospital for a day to be known as the "Teen Issues Forum." The students would experience seminar style presentations, a tour of some related units within the hospital and lunch. We arranged for knowledgeable speakers on each of the four subjects, and invited the students to attend. The response was overwhelmingly good. Speaker after speaker arrived and the students were both attentive and participatory. The three of us were sitting in the back of the assembly hall and, frankly, were reveling in our success. That feeling was only temporary as the front desk secretary came to inform us that our 'sex speaker' was not going to be able to make it to the seminar.

As we scrambled for a solution, I quickly came to the conclusion that one of us was going to have to do the sex talk. I shared this thought with my team members. They looked at me, they looked at each other and, as if they just realized they were both nuns, responded with "Well don't look at us". Being married and the father of three made me the new seminar "sexpert" by default.

It was a near death experience, addressing over eighty 8th grade students about sex and sexuality. I was terrified and I have absolutely no recall of what I said that day, but I remember the kids laughing and asking a lot of questions. The post-event survey comments were very positive and the nuns assured me that I did a great job. It didn't matter what they said. I was hooked. I knew this is what I should be doing.

It was not long until the program was being requested by every Catholic elementary school in Stark County. We were able to accommodate that demand by holding multiple forums throughout the school year. After a year of operating the program that way the public schools began to call, and not just one or two of them. A lot of them. This we could not handle. The average Catholic school has at most two 8th grade classes consisting of no more than 20 students per class. In fact, many of the schools had just one 8th grade. Public schools were a different matter entirely. Canton City schools for example average eight to ten eighth grade classes with at least 22 students per class. And Canton City Schools has four middle schools. Canton City is just one of seventeen public school districts in our county. The hospital simply could not handle numbers like this.

We decided to take the show on the road. Our outside presenters were already in most public schools. D.A.R.E. handled the drugs and alcohol presentations, the American Cancer Society and the American Heart Association had the smoking issue covered, and various local police departments handle the issues of guns and violence. What remained was the abstinence presentation. It was all ours and it was not long until we were taking our show on the road.

The demand for in school abstinence presentations surprised me. For so long it seemed everyone just ignored the problem, but once one school district had the nerve to face the problem the others fell like dominoes. I must give my former employers at the hospital a lot of credit. They hired me to do fundraising and here I was spending half my time talking about sex in area schools.

In 1995 a funny thing happened to my Catholic Hospital. It became the first in the nation to become a 'for-profit' entity by partnering with Columbia-HCA. Well, in case you are unaware, hospitals that are 'for-profit' no longer require the services of a fund development department. So, the week before Christmas in 1995 my department was eliminated. Merry Christmas. The good news was that a very savvy executive director of a local social service organization knew a good thing when he saw it. Dan Fuline, who is still the executive director of Community Services of Stark County, Inc. adopted the Marriage First Program along with it's sole presenter, me.

Since January of 1996 the Marriage First Program has prospered. Up and down funding has been the only fly in the ointment. Program growth required me to oversee a parade of prospective abstinence presenters. In case you are the least bit curious, it takes a very unique person to be able to talk openly and honestly about sex to hundreds of teens a week. So many people have such good intentions. But it is tough and the kids sensing any chink in the armor, will eat you alive. Ultimately, a young, newly hired employee begged for a chance to join the Marriage First Program. Frankly, I found her a bit annoying. She looked like she was about 16, and to be honest I did not think she had a prayer.

In order to shut her up, I agreed and then proceeded to send her to the toughest school in the entire county. I fully expected her to return with her tail tucked between her legs and absolutely no desire to continue. Imagine my surprise when Jen returned, jumped atop my desk, and proclaimed her absolute love for the program.

We have worked together ever since. We ultimately expanded programming to span from fourth grade through high school. We have a web site that gets over 8,000 hits a month, even though it is marketed solely in Stark County. For a time we had a pretty decent little radio show called "Answers – the call in questions and answer show for and about teens." We ran a very successful billboard campaign that so riled the local Planned Parenthood organization, that they responded with a billboard campaign of their own, featuring, believe this or not, a cross between a super hero and a hooker, known as 'Reality Girl'.

Suffice it to say that our Marriage First Program has been modeled in communities across the country. We have been independently and repeatedly evaluated and are proud to share our outcomes with anyone who will ask. We absolutely love the interaction with the students and live for the moments when we manage to get through to the hardest cases of all. By contrast however, we are greatly saddened when our information reaches the students too late or is simply ignored. We have heard more than once, "If only I could have heard you guys last year." The Marriage First Program is working hard to make sure that does not happen again.

What follows here is the crux of our presentation to the students, and some of their questions and comments in response to that presentation.

The Basic Truths

When speaking to a group of skeptics, it can be quite challenging to gain their acceptance. Any and all attempts to fool, cajole, or coerce them was met with undeniable resistance. As someone new to the game of presenting to young people, I had some difficulty in finding my way. Try as I might, I was unable to land upon a strategy that would sufficiently captivate my audience. One day, out of total desperation, and at the near end of the school year I decided to try the unthinkable. The truth.

While I thought I was talking to the students about 'abstinence until marriage' in reality I was talking to them about sex. It became almost immediately clear to me as to why I was garnering absolutely no credibility with the students. The bottom line was that I was trying to get them to delay or to discontinue having sex. Yet I had to admit that sex is good. In fact, sex is very good.

So there you have my dilemma. How could I tell the truth about sex, and still find a way to convince the virgins among them to continue waiting and the experienced among them to discontinue sexual activity? I did not take the time to develop a strategy. It was getting down to the wire as year one of this crazy journey was drawing to a close. I was desperate.

The following day I was scheduled to present at one of our two local Catholic High Schools. I wondered if this was really the place to dust of my all-new, truth filled presentation. In the end, I decided it was now or never and girded myself for the next day's presentations.

We were scheduled for four presentations that day and I barely had time to warn my program partner of the impeding change in our presentation. I basically told her to hold on and follow my lead. She always hated it when I threw her a curve, but something had to be done. So there, in front of two-dozen Catholic high school freshmen, I started the first of what has become hundreds of truth filled presentations.

"Hi, I'm Ray, and this is Jen" I began. "We are here to talk about sex. I love talking about sex. I love talking about sex almost as much as I love having sex. Since it would be completely inappropriate to actually have sex in front of a classroom full of students, then all I am left with is talking about it." Before I knew it I was in over my head. The truth just rolled off of my tongue much faster than I could discern what I should be saying and what I should not be saying. Much to the shock and utter dismay of my presentation partner, I rolled on. "Sex is good. It is designed to be that way. In fact, if your parents are home alone, well, they could just be…" It was at this point that my very sly smile conveyed the true meaning of my words.

My thoughts were interrupted by the decidedly clear sounds of moans and groans from the students and from my co-presenter as well. Those moans told me they were listening! I looked them over and they were staring very intently, actually hanging on my every word. I could not resist taking it one step further. "In fact, if your grandparents are home alone…" They were still listening, and the moans and groans multiplied with that revelation.

The students were either completely enraptured by my words or they were in total shock. In any case, I had their attention.

The truth will not only set you free, it will set you on the right path if you are trying to reach a group of young people. So from that moment on it was the truth or nothing. Besides, as much as I wanted to talk kids out of engaging in premature sexual behavior I had no desire to make use of scare tactics. Instead, I decided the truth along with 'care tactics' was the way to go.

So, in no particular order, here are the truths that make up the introductory component of the 'Marriage First' Presentation.

1) **Sex is good. It is very good.** (And where allowed by law, we even share that God designed it to be that way). We make no attempt to tell kids that sex is bad. Because it is not. It is normal. It is required for the procreation of life. It is supposed to be fun and it is supposed to feel good.

2) **Nothing comes without a price, and the better something is the higher the price.** Steak costs more than a hot dog, and a Corvette costs more than a Cavalier. If you want a really good steak you (or someone else) is going to have to pay for it. Sex, in my opinion is way better than steak and way better than a Corvette. I wouldn't trade away my sex life for either one, and I'm over fifty! But, it has a price. Physically, there can be a pregnancy, disease, or other

health complications. Emotionally, there can be distress or heartbreak. Financially there can be the cost of raising a baby or the cost of treating STDs. The potential costs of sexual activity seem to climb in inverse proportion to the age and maturity level of the individuals involved.

3)   **About half of American kids have sex prior to high school graduation, which in turn means about half of the kids in America have decided to wait.** More to the point, everybody is NOT doing it. To watch today's movies and television shows you would think that absolutely everyone on earth is having sex a couple dozen times a day. Of course, almost all movie and television sex is the total bomb, completely thrilling and without a single negative consequence. It is little wonder that so many of our young people are operating under the mistaken assumption that 'everybody is doing it'.

4)   **Everyone deserves a good, make that terrific, sex life.** I absolutely believe this. If it can be good for some it should be good for all. Unfortunately, so many young people have gotten sex all tangled up with worry, guilt, pain, doubt, and disease that it has become, for them, anything but good.

5)   **Good sex is worry free.** No one should have to worry about getting caught by their parents. No one should have to worry about getting a bad reputation or catching a disease. No one should have to worry if their actions may jeopardize their educational and career goals.

6)   **Good sex is guilt free.** No one should have to be concerned about violating their personal moral or religious beliefs. No one should have to wonder if they have just, in fact, cheated on their future husband or wife.

7)   **Good sex is pain free.** This is a statement more about emotional pain than physical pain. No one should have to go through being sexually involved with someone only to find out later that they were being used.

8)   **Good sex is doubt free.** A degree of commitment exhibited in the form of marriage helps make the complete physical surrender of one's self a much easier thing to do. Sex before marriage brings with it doubt about whether or not that relationship has staying power.

9)   **Good sex is disease free.** There is absolutely nothing positive that comes from introducing a sexually transmitted disease into a relationship. There are so many unpleasant symptoms that come along with STDs. A good number of these will directly impair one's ability to enjoy sexual activity.

10)   **Finally, abstinence is the only 100 percent effective way to avoid the physical, emotional, social, financial, and, for some, the spiritual costs of premature sexual activity. Period.**

Why Wait?

In every class, in every presentation we let the students do most of the work. We spend a lot of time talking about the sex is good stuff. We admit that the media such as movies, television, MTV, BET, the Internet, and song lyrics all paint a convincing picture that sex is awesome. In fact, the average young person sees approximately 14,000 sexual encounters per year on television alone.

Fourteen thousand. I found that to be an astonishing number. I shared that number with my wife of nearly thirty years. We started to wonder about that number and we actually began calculating what it would take to actually have 14,000 sexual encounters in a single year. It quickly became apparent that it would take over 38 encounters every day, to reach 14,000 in a single year. Since the average married couple has sex less than twice per week it was apparent that we needed a new formula. So, using the new numbers of twice per week for 52 weeks per year, it would take just 134 years to reach the magic number of 14,000. The point is that the media portrays a pretty unrealistic and overwhelming picture of sexuality in America.

We acknowledge this influence on young people. We acknowledge that they all have friends or older siblings who are giving them all sorts of unsolicited information on sex and sexuality. So, with all this momentum directing young people to the inescapable conclusion that a sex filled life is the only way to go, why would any young person decide to wait?

It would be simple for us to rattle off the answers we already knew, or the ones the students have given us in the past, but we elected to let them tell us, one class at a time. Over the years we have gathered dozens of reason why young people do elect to wait. Following are the top twenty:

Pregnancy	Moral Values
STDs	Family
Parents	Not Ready
Religion	Fear of Reputation
Wait for Right One	School
Physical Harm	Career
Sports	Money
Responsibility	Goals
Want Stuff	Social Life
Emotional	Don't Know How
Consequences	

It is important to note that it is the students who developed this list. They are given liberty to explain further. What follows is a combination of their follow-up assertions and the facts as they relate to the above listed top twenty.

PREGNANCY -

"So, is it true you can't get pregnant if you do it standing up?"

It is quite amazing what young people do NOT know about pregnancy. Perhaps that explains why more than one million U.S. teens get pregnant every single year. For those who need the obvious explained to them – every single teen that experiences an unplanned pregnancy is female. Yet, somewhat surprisingly we find that girls are more misinformed about pregnancy and its 'causes' than the boys. Perhaps it is because girls are more reluctant to talk with their friends, to seek out the facts. Perhaps, and more likely, they fall prey to the rumors started and spread by the male half of the population. Rumors that if believed, would make the ultimate goal of having sex with a girl much easier to achieve.

We have encountered more than a small handful of girls who actually did believe that they would not get pregnant if they 'did it' standing up. Of course, there is simply no truth to that. While lying down might well facilitate the movement of sperm toward the egg, there is no evidence to support the theory that standing up will prevent pregnancy. We encounter this myth in almost every school we visit. It is not, however, the most common.

Without doubt, the myth that appears to have the most widespread acceptance is that girls cannot get pregnant in their first-ever sexual encounter. I can't even begin to guess the percentage of girls, and guys, who actually believe this to be true, but the number is considerable, making this perhaps one of the most dangerous of myths. Of course, if you are to believe the explanations of pregnant teens it would seem as if nearly all of them got that way during their first and only sexual encounter ever.

Many girls also operate under the assumption that they cannot get pregnant while on their period. While there are certainly times of the month at which a girl is more fertile than other times, the fact remains that a girl can get pregnant at any time of the month. This false sense of security is pervasive among young teens.

Many girls and guys for that matter continue to believe that a girl cannot get pregnant until she has experienced her first period. This might well explain the ever-increasing birth rate among pre-teens. It is hard to believe that girls could miss something so obvious. Their first period is a result of an egg that has been released and has sat ready for fertilization for several days.

So many girls are unaware of the risk of pregnancy from simple, non-orgasmic contact with males. We often get the question "What if he pulls out in time?" It is hard to believe that girls continue to believe that they are safe as long as their intercourse does not end in male orgasm. Girls, it seems, are easy prey for even the most ludicrous of stories. Some myths that are often believed include things such as the second and third male orgasms in the same day are free from sperm or that douching with Pepsi or Coca-Cola after sex is an effective way to prevent pregnancy. Some even believe that taking heavy doses of aspirin after sex will serve the same purpose.

There can be no confusion here. And in the classroom it is explained quite clearly. If a girl puts herself, or more specifically her genitals, into contact with semen, she can get pregnant at any time of the day, the week, the month and in any position they can think of. It is inconceivable that so many girls of middle and junior high school age have an incomplete understanding of human reproduction.

We once did a parent presentation at a local middle school. One father, who's only child was an 8th grade student, asked when would be the right time to have "the talk" with their daughter. I was a bit taken aback, and before I could think of a more diplomatic answer I told him that ten years ago would have been a good time. Generally though, we tend to inform parents that "the talk" is not an event and is in reality more of a process. There will be more on this in the chapter "Where Do Parents Fit In?" starting on page 109.

SEXUALLY TRANSMITTED DISEASES-

"If I don't have a condom, can I use a baggie?"

When I first began giving abstinence talks I was most concerned about pregnancy. I knew the social, emotional, physical, financial, and in some cases, the spiritual consequences of early sexual activity. But now, the story is a different one. STDs (sexually transmitted diseases) are by far my single biggest concern. And this consequence, unlike pregnancy, does not single out the females as the victims.

Depending on the source you use there are between 35 and fifty STD's. Some sources say there are hundreds. And in a way there are. Some diseases, like HPV (Human Papilloma Virus) have numerous possible strains. In the case of HPV alone that number is eighty. Whatever the number you use the fact is that about half of them are viral based with the other half being bacterial based. Viral based STDs such as HIV, Herpes, and HPV are incurable. Bacterial based diseases such as Syphillis and Gonorrhea can be cured.

STDs bring with them a host of problems. STDs can lead to cancer, blindness, insanity, genital warts, open sores, impotence, infertility, painful intercourse, painful urination, and even death. Outcomes from bacterial based STDs can be avoided if treatment begins in a timely manner. In the case of viral based STD's the symptoms can be managed, but the disease cannot be cured.

There are five things we tell every classroom regarding STD's. If you learn and apply this knowledge in an appropriate way you can avoid acquiring an STD.

STD "must know" rule #1

You cannot tell if someone has an STD.

I have no doubt that people, especially young ones, are convinced they "would know" if a sexual partner were infected with a disease. They selected their potential dates because they come from the 'right side of the tracks'. Perhaps the family has obvious financial resources. Perhaps the girl's father or mother is a doctor. They assume that clean clothes and good grooming habits would almost guarantee a disease free partner. It is simply not the case. So in lieu of actually knowing it would be nice if people had some sort of built in warning system. You see a girl you are interested in. You approach her and engage her in a rather encouraging conversation. All seems to be going well until you make your first physical contact. All of the sudden sirens begin wailing, lights begin flashing, and a deep, loud voice comes seemingly out of nowhere announcing "Warning! Warning! The person you are touching is infected with an STD!"

The fact is, people do not have a warning system. In fact, almost everyone who contracts an STD goes through a period of time between infection and realization. In the case of HIV/AIDS an infected person can be symptom free for up to ten years! With other STDs, the time between infection and the first appearance of symptoms can vary from mere weeks to many months and even years. All this time, an infected person can be running around thinking they are "Joe Healthy". Perhaps the saddest part of this is that they are contagious and can be unknowingly infecting people.

While some STDs do exhibit external symptoms such as open sores or genital warts, most exhibit no overt symptoms at all. Even those that do will lapse into occasional, symptom free periods of remission. In the case of women, who have internalized sex organs, many symptoms that might occur would do so internally, making them virtually unnoticeable. An infected person could stand before you as naked as a jaybird and you likely would have no idea they were infected. The only certain way to detect STDs is to be specifically tested for them. This is the point at which the story gets really disturbing. A fairly recent survey in Glamour Magazine indicated that the majority of people who actually knew they had an STD would lie in order to enhance their chances of having sex with a potential partner.

STD "must know" rule #2

Young people are not immune.

Young people are quite possibly in the best shape of their lives. They can run all day, and stay up all night. In fact, if need be, they pull back-to-back all-nighters. They can run fast, jump high, and throw far. Give them a basketball and a hoop and they can play all day and all night in all kinds of weather. I have very fond memories of playing basketball with my friends in the dead of winter. Outdoors. We would play until we could no longer feel our hands, our face, and other parts unmentionable.

All this activity, this lack of rest, was often fueled by snack food based nutrition. And yet, the machine just kept running. It would be easy to think that you could be immune from all sorts of medical mayhem. I get a cold now and I feel like I should check into the Mayo Clinic. Back then a cold was at best a minor annoyance. This physical prowess brings with it a sense of invulnerability.

The fact is over 12,000 American teens will catch an STD this year. Did I say year? Scratch that. I meant to say over 12,000 American teens will catch an STD this month. Did I say month? Scratch that too. No more fooling around with this statistic. The fact is that over 12,000 American teens will catch an STD today. 12,000 more will catch an STD tomorrow and the next day and the next. Every day, 365 days of the year, 12,000 U.S. teens are going to catch an STD.

Have I made my point? Twelve thousand kids are going to wake up and decide to catch an STD tomorrow. I say decide because STDs do not leap off of lockers, they do not come from toilet seats, and they are not airborne. The only way a teen can catch an STD is to have sexual contact with an infected person. On the other hand, the good news is that the vast majority of teens will not catch an STD tomorrow, or any day for that matter. If a teen chooses to abstain from sexual activity, then they will be safe from STDs.

So many think they are immune. They really do not think it will happen to them. We, as parents and educators, need to stress to our young people that they are not immune. I have found that young people, when presented with all the facts, tend to make fairly responsible choices.

STD "must know" rule #3

<u>STDs are fair.</u>

They do not care if you are black or white, or green or red for that matter. They don't care if you are short or tall, smart or stupid, fast or slow. They do not care if you come from wealth or if you come from poverty. It matters not to STDs whether you live in a big house with the three-car garage or a run-down apartment in a seedy part of town.

In this way you sort of have to admire STDs. They are an equal opportunity annoyer. They are not the least bit prejudiced. You might like to imagine those STD bugs checking out a potential victim and deciding whether or not to infect the person. "Oh no, we can't infect her, she is running for homecoming queen and open herpes sores all over her face will doom her chances". Or, "He looks like a good choice, but I hear he has a chance at a full ride scholarship to play football at Ohio State. We can't infect him, he'd fail his physical and lose his scholarship". Well, the truth is, STDs do not care if you are about to become the homecoming queen. They do not care that you have a chance to play for Ohio State.

They just don't care. This is precisely why we must!

STD "must know" rule #4

You can catch an STD by engaging in any kind of sexual
activity.

Oral sex, anal sex, genital touching, mutual masturbation,
and intercourse are ALL activities that can spread STDs.
Ten or so years ago we began to see a downturn in teen
pregnancy rates. In fact in 2001, 2002, and 2003 the vast
majority of U.S. states recorded record low teen pregnancy rates. Yet, disturbingly, the rate of STD infection
among teens continued to climb.

It only took health officials a short while to determine the
cause of this new trend. Young people were engaging in
alternative sexual behaviors. Not only did these behaviors ensure a reduced birthrate, they allowed girls the
chance to retain their 'virginity'. In fact many younger
girls who have engaged in alternative sexual behavior don't
believe they had sex at all.

How this transformation from an intercourse focused culture to one that became alternative centered is relatively
easy to discern. One reason is due to our own making.
We spend a lot of time with pregnancy prevention programming and spend little if any time discussing the dangers of alternative behaviors. A second and decidedly significant explanation lies at 1600 Pennsylvania Avenue and
squarely in the lap (excuse the pun) of former President
William Jefferson Clinton.

In reality, none of that matters now. What matters is that
we make a focused effort to let young people know the

risks associated with alternative sexual behavior. Any direct contact with an infected persons genital region, whether with the hand, the mouth, the genitals, or even an elbow can lead to the transmission of an STD. The leading STD's require only skin-to-skin contact with no exchange of body fluids needed to transmit the disease. The STDs too have adapted to the trend toward alternative sexual activity. As a result of oral sex there now exist esophageal strains of both HPV and gonorrhea.

Perhaps most disturbing is the trend toward anal sex. This is the single riskiest sexual behavior when it comes to the spread of STDs. Add to that the risk of other potential infections, the cause of which should be readily apparent. Disease and infection aside, there exists the opportunity for serious injuries as a result of this activity.

You may find this hard to believe, but there are a number of web sites that cater to young people, that advocate for mutual masturbation as a safe alternative to intercourse. Among these sites is Teenwire, which is not surprisingly funded by none other than Planned Parenthood. While I have to agree that mutual masturbation will not lead to a pregnancy there seems to be little concern for the possible spread of STDs that can occur with this behavior. Contrary to the case with HIV/AIDS, where an exchange of body fluids such as blood or semen must occur in order to spread the disease, the leading STD's require just skin-to-skin contact.

STD "must know" rule #5

<u>There is no such thing as safe sex.</u>

Back in the 1960's, the safe sex movement in the form of what was then called "safe sex education" made it's way into mainstream public schools. Today it is better known as comprehensive sex education. Back then the major focus was on the use of condoms. I must say, as a high school student back in the late 60's it was great to hear that we could have all the sex we wanted without fear of pregnancy or the transmission of a sexually transmitted disease. Of course, back then there were only two STDs of any note, syphilis and gonorrhea. Since both of those STDs were bacterial based, they were easily cured with a single shot of penicillin.

Of course, in the midst of the "Make Love Not War" generation, it was most heartening to be given the free pass. What struck me as sort of odd was that no one questioned this. Ours was the generation that questioned absolutely EVERYTHING. For some reason, however, we gave this presentation a free pass. No doubt it was so good we didn't want to mess up a good thing.

Of course I am sure you are familiar with the old saying, "If something appears to be too good to be true, it probably is". As it turns out, this was precisely the case here. It was too good to be true. In fact, the safe sex that was preached to me back in 1968, turned out to not be safe at all. Health educators can no longer use the words "safe sex" or "safer sex" when referring to sex with some form of available protection. But we believed. Boy did we believe.

Our teen pregnancy rate started to soar and continued to do so until we led the entire industrialized world in that category. As if that was not enough, STD infection rates climbed as well. More disturbingly, the number of significant STDs rose from those two in the late sixties to some 35 today.

Safe sex indeed! We were duped. Whether by design or by accident, we were horribly misled. I feel it also fair to put a good share of the blame on us as well. After all, we questioned everything 'the system' told us. But we did not question this. We liked this too much to question it and we should have. We surely should have.

So now, in 2005, we are faced with epidemic STD rates. Luckily, since the abstinence education movement began to gain steam in the 1990's the teen pregnancy rate has begun (and continued) a steady decline, reaching record low teen pregnancy rates the last several years. What it comes down to is that there is NO SUCH THING AS SAFE SEX.

Inherent failure rates aside, condoms offer virtually no protection against the leading STD. This is according to the Centers for Disease Control in Atlanta. Since HPV, Human Papilloma Virus, infects the entire genital region and requires only skin-to-skin contact for its transmission, it is easy to see why a condom will not do the job. In fact, you could wear the whole box and you would be no better off. All birth-control devices for women offer virtually no protection against STDs.

Can a condom help reduce the chance of a pregnancy occurring? Yes, it can. Is a condom 100% effective in preventing pregnancy? No, it is not. Can a condom reduce the chance of acquire HIV/AIDS? Yes, it can. Will a condom provide protection against HIV/AIDS 100% of the time? No, it will not. Can a condom protect against the spread of HPV and Herpes? Condoms are virtually useless in preventing the spread of these diseases. Perhaps this explains precisely why they are the two leading STDs.

Condom proponents like to hang their hat on the fact that condoms can offer protection against HIV/AIDS. I worry though that they seem unwilling to acknowledge that they are virtually useless against HPV. This is an important issue because over 97-percent of all cervical cancer cases in America are caused by HPV. This is not to say that everyone who catches HPV will get cervical cancer. This is to say that virtually all people who do have cervical cancer got it from an HPV infection. No HPV – no cancer!

I am at a loss as to why so many women back a comprehensive sex education program that does nothing to protect women from HPV. I am shocked that women continue to allow themselves to be victimized in this way. According to the National Cancer Institute (NCI), the average number of life years that a woman will lose to cervical cancer is 25.3. Why aren't women's groups everywhere making this their number one issue? In addition, the vast majority of HPV strains (there are about 80 of them) produce absolutely no symptoms in men.

If you have read this and conclude that you are still uncertain regarding the value, or lack thereof, of comprehensive sexual education be sure to check out page 123 and the "Case Against Condoms".

PARENTS-

"My parents are sooooo uncool, there is no way they know anything about sex."

Students commonly list parents as one of their top five reasons for delaying the onset of sexual activity. Sometimes, they explain, it is the fear of being caught. For the most part, however, they claim they do not want to disappoint their parents. Those should be some comforting words to most parents. Your kids do not want to disappoint you.

In fact in several recent studies evaluating the relative impact of the media, friends, teachers, and parents on young people, it was clearly learned that parents have the most influence! And this statistic holds true until your child is in their early 20's. There is, however, only one way to have an impact on your child when it comes to their sexual decision-making. You have to be willing to talk with them about your expectations. You have to be willing to show them that you do indeed know plenty about sex. I mean let's face it, your children have always suspected it. How else could they possibly explain their presence? Remember that children of all ages need guidelines. It is so much easier to live up to expectations if you know what those expectations are.

There is one word of warning here. All the talk in the world will be meaningless if you do not walk the walk. You cannot convincingly talk about the importance of abstinence until marriage if you happen to be a single parent who commonly entertains an overnight guest.

RELIGION-

"But my religion says we should love one another."

Every student seems to be aware that sex outside of marriage is frowned upon by most, if not all, major world religions. Every once in while we will hear that "we are supposed to love one another". Of course, the student making this statement already knows that love and sex are really two different things. For some though, religion is their guiding light. They do their best to honor their faith and they know that includes no sex before marriage.

I want to point out here that this is one of twenty reasons the students give us as reasons to delay the onset of sexual activity. Interestingly, public school students generally list religion as one of their top ten reasons. Students who attend faith-based schools generally list religion on their top twenty list, significantly lower than their public school counterparts. Since federally funded abstinence programs are not allowed to promote religion in the classroom, our only response to the students is that the vast majority of world religions, while having differing views on a variety of topics, agree that sex outside of marriage is a bad idea.

It does cause me to wonder how various religions cannot agree on who God is, or even how many gods there are, but can be in such accordance on this issue. Chapter IX will have a lot more to say on the relationship between abstinence until marriage and religion.

WAIT FOR RIGHT ONE –

"I think I will wait until I find the right one, the one I want to marry, but I still think a test drive is a good idea."

This is a case where the student was on the right track. I was just preparing to let loose with a beaming smile when the student unleashed that part of the sentence after the second comma. The majority of the class laughed and I am not even sure if he was being totally serious. The truth is though we have heard this kind of thinking before. I think it points out an area of confusion about human sexuality.

Many students have expressed the desire to wait for the "right one". However, a very high percentage of them have conveyed a sincere fear that they may learn too late that they are sexually incompatible with that partner. We spend a lot of time talking about some of the key ingredients to a successful long-term relationship. One of those keys is physical attraction. Let's face it, if you find your partner's appearance to be more repulsive than attractive, there really isn't much hope of long-term success.

What we try to convey to the students is that the physical attraction that draws you to someone is proof enough that there will be all the sexual chemistry that a couple will ever need to initiate a marital relationship. Young people must learn that waiting for the right one is not only a good idea, it is a great one. Parents need to share something of their knowledge of attraction and sexual compatibility. This is a case where the more that is said the better.

PHYSICAL HARM-

"It's my body and I will do what I want with it."

When the students list physical harm, they do not mean it in terms of the impact of STDs. They are referring to the physical impact of pregnancy on a young girl's body and the potential injuries that can sometimes occur with sexual activity. One thing they should perhaps consider is the possible physical harm that can easily befall a young man who is caught in the act by the girl's none-too-happy father.

Pregnancy in a young teen is especially hard on both the girl and the baby. The vast majority of low birth weight babies are born to teen mothers. It becomes readily apparent that this is not just a matter of a girl and her body. The teen years are not the best years to give birth. In many cases the girls are not even fully developed enough to deliver naturally. A C-section is major surgery and can present serious medical complications.

One thing that has always amazed me is the lack of consideration given by girls to the changes to their body. Our society is a very image conscious one. Girls especially, go to extreme lengths to enhance and maintain their appearance. During classroom presentations we share information about stretch marks and weight gain as well as other bodily changes. One of the most impactful things a mother can share with her daughter is her stretch marks. We have heard more than a couple of times, "My mom showed me her stretch marks and they are so gross I am never going to have kids." While that might be taking it too far, a little apprehension might be a good thing.

SPORTS-

"I ain't never seen a pregnant girl run the hurdles"

Well, neither in fact, have I. At least I have never seen a visibly pregnant girl. It is easy to see the connection between sports participation and not being pregnant. Girls know that pregnancy is in no way going to enhance their athletic performance. In fact they know that, certainly at the high school level, a pregnancy is a career closer. So it might not be at all surprising that girls who do not participate in school or club sports are three times more likely to experience an unplanned pregnancy. Of course, this is not to say that if you force your daughter to join a sports team that she will be risk free.

There have been no studies to determine if this reduced chance of pregnancy is simply due to the fact that these girls have less time on their hands or due more to the fact that these girls may be more goal oriented. Perhaps they understand the negative impact that a pregnancy will have on achieving their goals. At this point it does not matter. It is apparent that encouraging your daughters to pursue sports and other school activities certainly won't hurt.

What is often missed in the classroom discussion is the negative impact that an unplanned pregnancy might have on male student athletes. While the physical aspects of pregnancy certainly are not going to affect male students they should indeed be concern about the financial consequences. Most states now require that the father of a new-

born be identified. States now pursue these dads in order
to collect support for their child. The average young man
who gets a girl pregnant today will spend approximately
$157,000 on child support.

Many young men will not be able to handle the demands
of school, sports and work. Something has to give, and it
is usually sports. Hopefully, it can stop there, because the
next thing to go by the wayside is school and that creates
a whole new set of problems.

RESPONSIBILITY-

"It is no problem, if I have a baby I know my mom will help me raise it."

Thankfully, most students by far feared more that their parents would be more likely to 'kill them' then raise their children for them. Sometimes it is a good idea to remind students that it is okay to continue enjoying their life as a freeloader, as opposed to jumping into a world of responsibilities.

In a nice way, feel free to remind your children that life really does not get much easier than it is now. Most of their clothes are free. The same is true with their transportation, education, shelter, health care and food needs. Parents provide countless additional amenities such as money for entertainment, cell phones, vacations, and sometimes even a car.

I encourage young people to enjoy this ride as long as possible. I tell them it is okay to be freeloader because that is what a kid is supposed to be. I am also very clear in explaining that once you decide to engage in adult behavior you are setting yourself up for adult responsibilities.

When I graduated from college I entered the grown-up world rather quickly by getting married. After that, my father no longer picked up the tab for my food, clothing, and shelter. He no longer provided me with cars or gas money or insurance coverage or much else for that matter. All that fell, rather suddenly, to me. Frankly, I liked it better when dad was picking up the tab.

WANT STUFF-

"I will be able to get everything I need from the government."

As a part of my job, I also run a homeless shelter. Over 90 percent of the good folks in that shelter are in families that were started by unwed teen moms. Here is a news flash to everyone within reading distance: The government is no longer in the business of covering the life long expenses for you and your child. Public assistance has undergone an overhaul and while it still exists, it is no longer a long-term solution.

This is one time where I think that it is actually okay for a person to be selfish. I encourage young people to dream of attending college. I tell them to imagine driving the car of their dreams. I ask them to share a favorite vacation destination or a dream trip of a lifetime. All these things cost money.

We spend a lot of time discussing the value of completing that high school education. Following high school a young person can begin their career or choose to continue with their education. In any case, eventually, they will realize a financial reward that will allow them to acquire some of the 'stuff' they desire. An unplanned pregnancy will do little to help them acquire, travel, or attend.

EMOTIONAL CONSEQUENCES –

"Is it true that girls like to have some sort of emotional connection to a guy before they, you know, do it?"

I work for a social service agency. While I am not a counselor, I have had the opportunity to speak to many of our counselors about matters of teen sexuality. We also operate a web page that is set up to answer the concerns and questions of young people everywhere.   Many, many people seek counseling every year because they have been in an intimate physical relationship with someone only to find themselves dumped in short order. They are feeling used and abused, and they are also about 95 percent female.

Our web site reflects a similar pattern.   There are a lot of questions from guys about STD's and pregnancy, but very few questions from guys about being sexually misused and then summarily dumped. We do get questions from girls about STDs and pregnancy, but we get a whole lot more about the emotional damage they are dealing with as a result of a sexual relationship gone bad.

Guys and girls think about sex very differently. For girls it is still primarily a way to enhance an emotional connection. For guys, especially of high school age, it is a physical expression, more likely one of lust. What I have found to be most surprising, is that young men appear to have very little realization that the girls are emotionally invested in their sex partners. They seem surprised to learn that the girls they dump suffer emotional scars. Simply making them aware appears to make a difference.

MORAL VALUES –

"Some times, after sex with my boyfriend, I feel guilty. Is this a bad thing?"

A lot of students mention that they think a lot of their peers do not have sex before marriage because of their personal morals. Most studies indicate that young people primarily acquire their moral code from their parents. For those of you who have taken the time to instill a sense of morals in your child you have my eternal gratitude. You have just done your part to make the world a better place to live.

Sadly though, it seems just as many parents feel no responsibility to instill moral values in their children. In fact, there is now institutional support for parents who do not instill morals in their children. I attended a three-day social worker seminar about a year ago, where the speaker actually intoned that parents have no right to force their moral beliefs on their children.

I wish I could tell you what evidence he offered to back up that claim, but to be honest with you I walked out of the room. And as if that was not enough, I loudly muttered an "Oh, Brother" as I made for the door. After the next segment of the seminar, and during the morning break that speaker sought me out. He wanted to let me know that he thought it was rather rude of me to make negative comments while walking out of his session. I informed him that while most people might apologize at this point, that would not be the case with me, as my parents never bothered to instill me with any sort of behavioral guidelines. Frankly, based on his assertions, I would have thought he would have been a lot more understanding than he was.

The bottom line is simple. If you want your children to have a moral code, it has to come from you. These values are imprinted at a very young age. The process of instilling a moral code cannot happen in school. It is too late for that. It is up to the parents to do the job. Of course, you can choose to believe this nonsense that you have no right instilling your morals, your values on your children. Essentially you will raise a child who will have no way of discerning right from wrong.

At this point society will impose its values on your child. There will be consequences for unacceptable behavior. I have seen the way these parents respond when their child is continually sent home from school with notice of misbehavior, detention and the like. They blame the teacher, the coach, the school. When their child later has difficulty maintaining employment, it is always the employer's fault. When they run afoul of the law the police and the judges are to blame. It is an endless saga of diffusing the responsibility that, in fact, lies with their parents.

Instilling a moral code gives your child a sense of direction. It will help them make good decisions for themselves. Instill your morals and values for your child out of love before the state imposes theirs, without the benefit of a loving touch.

FAMILY-

"My mom won't be mad at me if I get pregnant. She got pregnant in high school too. But, boy will my grandma ever be mad!"

Almost every class of students lists parents ahead of other family. Other family though, still makes a big impact. We ask the female students to imagine having to tell your parents and other relatives that you are pregnant. We ask the boys to imagine telling their parents and other relatives that they got their girlfriend pregnant.

Their responses are quite touching. While they all acknowledge that telling their parents would be extremely difficult they seemed decidedly more saddened by the prospect of breaking the news to their favorite aunt or their favorite grandparent. I have actually seen girls tear up at the thought of having to inform their younger sister that they were pregnant.

We explored this outpouring and tried to figure out what exactly was the cause of this response. What we discovered was pretty darned insightful. Parents, it seems, know that there are ups and downs to the job of parenting. So, while telling mom and dad presents a very fear filled moment, they know their parents are there for them. When it comes to other relatives they do not share the burden in the same way. Their favorite aunt or grandparent has always been the provider of good times. They definitely do not deserve to be hurt. Parents, it seems, know that this comes with the territory. When it comes to younger siblings, it seems most girls dread being a poor example.

NOT READY-

"Just exactly what is the right age to begin having sex?"

We get this question a lot. I am glad we do. It is evidence that young people are curious about doing the right thing. They seem amazed when I tell them I honestly believe that there is no right age for the onset of sexual activity. There probably exists the rare 16-year old who is already the right age to begin sexual activity and there are equally as many 40-year olds who are still not ready to begin engaging in sexual activity.

There really is no magic number. It is based more on preparedness than on longevity. It is as simple as this. When two people are in a position to handle the possible outcomes from sexual activity then they are ready to actually have sexual activity. By 'possible outcomes' we are referring primarily to STDs and Pregnancy. And by 'ready' we mean in a position to handle the social, physical, emotional, and financial aspects of the outcome.

For example, in the case of a pregnancy, 'ready' means educated, employed and in a position to provide your newly created life with food, clothing, shelter, medical care, transportation and ultimately, entertainment and education.
While it might rankle the feathers of some of our left thinking social scientists, it would also be nice if your relationship with the co-creator of this new life were strong enough to provide your new child with a stable, two-parent home.

FEAR OF GETTING A BAD REPUTATION-

"Guys just love slutty girls, so I really hope that is the way they think of me."

Contrary to the young lady's thoughts expressed above, the vast majority of girls worry that they will acquire a bad reputation. Young girls, in the 10-14 year old age range seem totally unaware that a bad reputation can be acquired with promiscuous behavior. As mentioned earlier, many girls that age who are engaged in sexual activity are operating under the belief that they are not having sex.

When girls reach 15 years of age they seem to be much more concerned about gaining a bad reputation. While some girls, like the one quoted above, seem to find some odd benefit in having a bad reputation, most girls, sexually active or not, do not want a bad reputation.

You may have noticed the discussion here is focused on the girls. Sadly, reputation is just one of many areas in which the girls pay a bigger price for their sexual involvement than do the boys. The nicknames that girls with a bad reputation do acquire are very unpleasant, even to the point that I am uncomfortable repeating them here. Boys, when they are thought to be sexually active can also acquire nicknames. Most though almost border on complimentary. Player. Stud. Pimp Daddy.

Is it fair that sexually active guys seem to get a free pass while girls take a pretty serious hit? No, it is not fair, but the fact is, life is not fair. The sooner your children learn this fact the better!

SCHOOL-

"What the heck is the big deel about getting an educaton anyways?"

We received the above comment on a post presentation survey form. It was from a high school junior. Since the students themselves give us this list we know that they know an education is very important. Based on the quote above I think we have to thank God that most young people do understand the value of education even if they are not paying attention in spelling class.

Specifically, a teen that has an unplanned pregnancy is seven times more likely to end up on public assistance than to ever attend college. The United States Department of Health and Human Services indicates that an unplanned teen pregnancy is one of the leading indicators of life long poverty. This poverty is a direct outgrowth of the interruption of their education.

As I stated earlier, I have the distinct pleasure (and I mean this) of running a homeless shelter for single women and families. Over 90 percent of the families that stay in our shelter are families started by unmarried teen moms.

Frankly there are so many studies that make the link between a lack of education and lifelong poverty that this book is not big enough to list them all. Some of those studies are quick to point out that, while girls generally are more impacted by an unplanned pregnancy, guys too can suffer a negative impact. Young men, facing the cost of supporting a family, are often forced to drop out of school in order to meet that need.

CAREER-

"So, are you saying that the only way to have a good career is to get a college degree?"

In fact we never indicate that the only path to a successful career is attending and graduating from college. We give equal weight to a two-year degree, a technical school diploma, and even a high school diploma. What we do try to convey, is that regardless of your educational aspirations the best way to a good career is to not saddle yourself with an unplanned pregnancy until you get your career on track.

A woman with a high school degree is very employable, especially in the entry-level employment market. That is the good news. The bad news is that entry-level jobs rarely provide a living wage. Most singles employed at this level continue living with their parents or find a roommate to share expenses with. Given enough time an entry-level employee can advance on the job and enhance their earnings to the point they will earn a living wage.

The option of continued schooling remains a viable one and in some cases the employer may assist in absorbing the cost of continued education. However, should a high school educated woman have a child that requires paid childcare her options become severely limited? Entry-level jobs are barely enough for one person to live on, let alone a family. What generally follows is a forced dependence on a male provider. While this can actually work out, more likely is the birth of even more children and an ever-increasing financially forced dependence on a male provider.

MONEY-

"Isn't that what the government is for?"

When it comes to money, kids actually have a lot of common sense. They know for example, that they would much rather spend their money on an I-Pod than on three boxes of disposable diapers and a case of formula.

Many of them know the financial impact of a new born. Many share stories from their own home or from older siblings on the financial havoc wrought by a newcomer. They have seen the once comfortable life of their older sister thrown into turmoil with the cost of medical care, formula, baby clothes, baby furniture, diapers and a myriad of other expenses.

What is odd is that the kids from the upper end of the socioeconomic spectrum seemed to have a much keener sense of the financial impact caused by the arrival of a baby. Students from the lower end of the socioeconomic spectrum mentioned money as a reason to delay sexual activity about one-fourth as often as the students from the upper end of the spectrum.

Many shared the opinion expressed above. They have a belief that the government will take care of them and their baby. As one young girl said "they have to, because we are young". The fact is, the welfare rules have changed and any help from the government will be short-lived. The impact will not be a positive one. According to HRSA, an unplanned teen pregnancy is the leading indicator of life long poverty.

GOALS-

"Can having a baby really get in the way that much?"

Thankfully, I guess, a lot of kids are selfish today. They have a lot that they want to accomplish and just a lot that they want. They want stuff like cars, and trips, and motorcycles. They want accomplishments like education, more education, and a prestigious career. And gratefully, they want a life. They want a happy marriage complete with kids and a pet schnauzer.

That is the good news. The bad news is a lot of our young people today are impatient. I know this was probably the same thing said about my generation, and the one before mine, and the one before that. Every generation it seems wants to accelerate the achievement curve.

There are certain things that they know will take time. Finishing college for example. But there are other things they want right away. A new car would be a great example of this. If you don't believe me, take a drive through the student parking lot at your local high school. Then, on your way out to the road, make sure you take a spin through the teacher's lot. I think you will see what I mean.

It seems the more fun something is, the more impatient they become. We already know that sex is fun, and it seems that this is one thing that kids have a very split opinion on. About half of high school kids in America give in to the temptation and have sex before graduation. The other half of America's high school students wait. It does seem, that the goal of achieving a high school diploma is incentive enough for some students to wait.

Ten years ago the percentage of students who decided to have sex prior to graduation was about 72 percent. For those of you mathematically challenged, like myself, that means just 28 percent were at least waiting to graduate. Things have changed in the last ten years, which coincidentally is just about the same span of time that the abstinence movement has been spreading.

Abstinence programs across the country vary somewhat in their content. Some lean heavily on the consequences of STDs. Some are primarily pregnancy prevention programs. Some take a more global approach – my program fits into this category. But whether it be the STDs or an unplanned pregnancy or something else altogether, there is one thing they all have in common. It is that the consequences of sexual activity will stand between you and your goals.

Pregnancy can prevent the completion of high school or college. Acquiring an STD can interfere with a sports scholarship or the future ability to have those children.
Families, who have generally stood along side, providing assistance and guidance, might well toss in the towel when they find out their young son or daughter is sexually active. The emotional toll of a breakup after a relationship has become physically intimate can have a very negative impact on future relationships.

The decisions kids make today don't affect just today. The decisions young people make don't affect just them. They affect their future and the people around them.

SOCIAL LIFE-

"I don't think my friends would mind if I brought my baby along to the movies."

Right now your young person likely has the best social life ever. There is always something going on in high school. There are sporting events. Concerts. Plays. Dances. Dating. For the average high school student, the lack of responsibility in their lives allows them full opportunity to enjoy all the social life that high school, and college for that matter, has to offer.

The fact that they are not tied down with children allows them to take advantage of social opportunities on the spur of the moment. One young man, after hearing this explanation, said he was getting the impression that getting pregnant while still in high school could rob a girl of her freedom. I could not have said it better. Not only can an unplanned pregnancy rob a girl of her freedom, but it can do the same for a guy as well.

If you have children, you know what I am talking about. My presentation partner used to be a skier. I say used to be because she hasn't been on a ski slope since she got pregnant with her first son about four years ago. She and her husband Mark were avid skiers while they were dating, and they were just as avid after they married. They would either plan events months in advance, or would just decide on a Friday morning to spend the weekend on the slopes. Sure they had jobs and household responsibilities but they were always able to work in a ski trip. After all, the job was only a five-day a week commitment and household chores could always wait.

Children are a seven-day a week commitment and the chores involved in their upbringing cannot be put on hold. Now a ski trip involves setting up overnight baby sitting AND finding the money needed to afford the ski trip. Funny how the cost of formula, diapers, baby clothes and furniture quickly supplant the cost of a lift ticket. It is not just about weekend ski trips either. When high school kids decide to attend a movie a friend may get all of ten seconds notice. Most kids will yell downstairs and ask if it is okay to go catch a movie with their buddies. When mom or dad answer back that all is okay, the evening is underway.

When a high school student has and parents a baby, she will experience a very dramatic change in her social life. Oh, sure her friends will call her initially. They will ask her if she wants to go to a movie. But, when she turns them down time and again because she cannot find a sitter or has no money left for a movie ticket, her friends will soon stop calling. This is a shocking change for a girl who months earlier had total freedom of movement. It is sad really. Think back on how much you enjoyed that simple freedom. Think of the potential resentment that one might harbor if that freedom were suddenly gone. Our kids are already growing up too fast and this is one case where our young people could use a little help. Sometimes the simplest explanation of their current level of freedom, and the changes to that freedom that likely would occur in the event of a pregnancy can have a very big impact. If there is one thing a young person can relate to, it is the potential loss of their freedom to come and go as they please.

DON'T KNOW HOW–

"Well, to be honest I think I would like to give it a try someday. But I just don't known how."

In a refreshing moment of complete honesty a middle school student at a local city school shared, in front of his entire class, the above thought. I admire his bravery but question his discretion. As you might imagine the class broke into an uproar of laughter. I felt a little bad for the kid but he seemed to thoroughly enjoy the reaction he had wrought.

What is bizarre is that so many young people think they know all there is to know about sex and sexuality. Yet, in general, they exhibit an incredible lack of knowledge in everything from teen pregnancy, to STDs, to the sex act itself.

While most kids want to pass themselves off as some sort of expert in the field of human sexuality, there are some who are willing to ask the questions that need answering. It never ceases to amaze me at the way the so-called experts in every class crane their necks to catch every syllable of my response.

It is apparent that all students are thirsty for more knowledge, and correct information regarding teens and sexuality. So many kids base their knowledge on what is fed to them by their somewhat unknowing friends. Even worse, are the numbers of kids who feel they are experts in human sexuality because of what they have learned through their viewing of pornography.

The Internet has made pornography so accessible I cannot imagine even one student being able to avoid it entirely. In the old days, when I was a young teenager you would have felt like you had struck gold just to have come across a two year old, severely dog eared copy of a *Playboy* magazine. Back then a *Playboy* had a lot of stories, a lot of letters, some racy comics, and a couple dozen pictures of naked women, in a series of mundane poses.

The women were beautiful, and could possibly have created false expectations of what all women would and should look like, but beyond that they seem pretty harmless by today's standards. Online your child can find pornographic photographs and stories that go well beyond that *Playboy* magazine of forty years ago. Group sex, incest, bestiality, same-sex unions, sado-masochistic behavior, and fetishes abound.

This is by NO means an accurate portrayal of sex in America, or anywhere else for that matter. It is a danger that any young person might think this is truly the way to express oneself sexually. Even more disturbing are the number of young males who are becoming addicted to pornography. They utilize it as a source of arousal and the focal point of masturbatory fantasies. Over time, as desensitization occurs, the young males turn to harder and harder forms of pornography.

This causes two significant problems. A connection to more bizarre forms of sexual behavior is made with the ever-present chance that a young man will actually believe this is normal sexual behavior. The second problem occurs in males who are obsessed with self-pleasure. I once met an 8th grade boy who attended a local private elementary school. His fellow students got me aside and told me I needed to have a conversation with him. They told me he was "really weird" and was "constantly touching himself in class". When class was over, I told the kids I would hang around for while if anyone needed to talk privately. Much to my relief, the young man in question did approach me. He wondered if he was a bad kid because he masturbated.

I told him I did not think he was a bad kid for masturbating, and asked him why he was asking. He confessed that he did it "a lot". I guess I probably should have known better, but I asked him how much a lot was. He told me he masturbated eight to ten times a day! His only worry was that he might be hurting himself. I have had this kind of question before, but my answer never seemed more applicable than to this young man.

I explained that sex is really something designed to be shared by a man and a woman. You have to admit that the parts do fit so nicely together! I further explained that his masturbation habit would probably serve to make him a lousy lover. A good lover knows how, or at least makes a tremendous effort, to please his partner. He, and in fact most guys, want to fancy themselves quite the lover.

They seemed a bit perplexed that being sexually savvy extends well beyond ones own body and one's own pleasure. It is at this point that we learn that one outspoken lad is not the only one who "does not know how."

Why Go Ahead?

Just as we ask the students why they would wait to delay the onset of sexual activity, we also ask why some choose to go ahead. We wonder aloud as to why young people would ignore all those reasons to wait and all that risk, and decide to go ahead anyway. I sincerely want to know what motivates young people to realize that the risk levels are pretty daunting, and yet decide to go ahead anyway. I will be honest with you. Sometimes it takes a bit of time to extract reasons from kids as to why some young people choose to wait. However, when we ask them why some students decide to go ahead, the answers come at an alarming rate.

I can barely keep up with them as I try to record their answers on the board. Following are the top twenty:

Peer Pressure	Feels Good
Hormones	Love
Prove Manhood	Keep Boy/Girl Friend
Already Did It	Revenge
Rebellion	Bored
To Fit In	To be Popular
Media Pressure	Poor Role Models
Immune	Curiosity
To Relieve Stress	Make Boyfriend Happy
Drugs/Alcohol	Everybody Is Doing It

What follows are the explanations we give to dispel each and every justification the students give for initiating sexual activity. We know that for them, these answers are real and honest so we take them seriously. That is not to say that we do not have a little fun in making our point.

PEER PRESSURE

"I know this is the number one reason for doing the wrong thing."

Peer pressure in the area of sex, is primarily a girl-to-girl or a guy-to-guy thing. When the pressure comes to sex, it appears that your peers are gender specific. Kids do know that peer pressure is the number one reason for doing the wrong thing. What they, and many other people fail to realize, is that peer pressure could be a good thing as well.

Smoking cessation campaigns of a decade ago that proved most successful among young people were campaigns that featured young people as the front men and women in the campaign. Young actors were used in the advertising and grass roots mobilization of thousands of young people made the difference. The perceived peer pressure generated by this campaign produced dramatic reductions in the number of new teen smokers. Kids can influence their friends from engaging in threatening or dangerous behavior. They can encourage their buddies to show up at school, to do their homework, to turn their keys over and not drive while drunk.

However, when it comes to sex it seems most of the peer pressure leans away from the path that is safe and consequence free. The desire to have sex often times overwhelms the desire to remain safe and risk free. Generally speaking, young people are optimists and just do not think it will happen to them. The consequences of sexual activity are not as immediate as those for driving under the influence.

As more and more young people are made aware of the consequences of sexual activity, I have to believe that the peer pressure regarding sex might well swing to encouraging the safer behavior of abstinence. In fact, many schools have 'virginity clubs' or 'chastity clubs' where like-minded students can encourage one another to remain abstinent until marriage. It really is amazing how capable our young people are at making a good decision when they have all the needed information. Kids, who decide to commit to abstinence and surround themselves with like-minded friends, will have a much greater chance of success than those who don't.

One of the strangest motivating factors among girls encouraging other girls to engage in sexual activity is more like a case of "misery loves company". Many girls who have decided to have sex have almost instantly regretted their decision. Since they see no way to take it back, they simply determine that it is easier to drag others down with her.

The truth is, this motivation for pressuring one's friend into having sex should be an easy one to eliminate. It is here that the concept of "secondary virginity" comes into play. Beginning on page 76 is a further exploration of this concept.

The best way to lose the negative impact of peer pressure is to turn it around into a positive force. This is accomplished through a continual stream of educational presentations about the truth when it comes to sex and consequences.

FEELS GOOD

"If something feels good, then why is it such a bad idea to have sex?"

We get this. Sex does feel good. It is supposed to feel good. Interestingly, this answer comes almost exclusively from guys. Sure, once in a great while we will get a girl that lists this among her reasons as to why young people decide to go ahead and have sex. Even then though, the girl is thinking of it in terms of her boyfriend.

What is sad is that not only do very few girls list this among their reasons for going ahead, but also many in fact report that they do not like sex. This should really come as no surprise. Girls and guys have a very different perspective when it comes to sex. I know this is a generalization and that there are exceptions to the rule. Guys, especially the young ones all tanked up on testosterone, think of sex as a physical act. It is for physical pleasure, and that is that. Thoughts of emotional bonding, love, starting a family are very far from their mind. Girls on the other hand, see sex as a very emotional activity. They crave the closeness and cherish the feeling of being wanted.

Boys will almost always experience pleasure when having sex. Most don't worry that the girl will not love them in the morning. They don't worry that they will get pregnant. Boys don't worry that they might gain a bad reputation. The achievement of an orgasm, is really all it takes for most young males to find sex to be an enjoyable experience.

Girls on the other hand, do worry about getting pregnant, about whether the guy really loves them, about gaining a bad reputation. Girls want sex to be an emotional experience. They want to feel wanted and need to feel needed. With all this worry and doubt, it is little wonder that many girls actually claim they do not like sex. I get a lot of e-mails every month from girls who wonder if there is something wrong with them because they do not enjoy sex.

There are so many reasons that the problem is not with them. It is normal for them to expect some security as a result of giving their body over to someone else. There is nothing wrong with a girl who worries to the point that she is unable to enjoy sex. In fact, there is everything right with her. Everything inside of her heart and mind are telling her that having sex at this point in her life is a bad idea, and her body responds accordingly.

Guys, young guys primarily, don't have too much trouble worrying about all the things girls worry about. They seem to spend all their time worrying about themselves. It does not take much in the way of technique for a guy to have a great time sexually. It does not even take much in the way of time. Girls however require both technique and time. Put those very different sexual expectations together and there is bound to be someone in that pairing who is going to come away disappointed.

The real problem here is that, generally speaking, kids think sex is awesome. It is what they see on television, in the movies, in their music videos, basically everywhere. As you can imagine, they are all eager to try it. For the boys, it very easily lives up to their expectations. For girls, it very easily ends up being a big disappointment.

This leads to an even bigger question. If girls report that they do not like it, then why do they continue having sex? Part of the answer lies with the fact that some girls will do just about anything to keep their boyfriend happy. (More on this in a subsequent section of the book). In other cases the girls really do believe the fault lies with them. Their solution to the problem is to just keep trying. They assume that with more effort and more trying on their part it will just get better.

What is perhaps most sad is that girls begin associating sex, which is supposed to be a good thing, with fear and worry and guilt, which are bad things. The problem with this sort of association is that it can have a long-term, even life-long impact. It is called conditioning. Back in the seventies there was a pretty famous smoking cessation experiment. Subjects enrolled in a residential program that was designed to help them quit smoking. The program was one of the most successful smoking cessation programs ever developed.

The program was successful because it associated something the client liked, smoking, with something most people do not like, throwing up. Clients were wired with a remote control injection device. It contained ipecac, which when injected would cause the client to throw up almost instantly. Personnel would follow the clients 24/7 via surveillance cameras. Whenever they put a cigarette to their lips the staff member would hit the remote and the smoker was doubled over in seconds, losing the night's dinner. In the second week of treatment, the clients would just so much as look at a cigarette and they would soon be throwing up. Well as you can imagine, the vast majority of the clients in this program stopped smoking. In fact, studies of these same individuals many years later showed them going to extreme lengths to avoid cigarettes. They would show them walking down the street, just minding their own business. A smoker would be heading at them from the opposite direction. The smoking cessation clients would cross the street to avoid going anywhere near the smoker.

When asked about their behavior by the film crew they were totally unaware of their actions. Their decision to cross the street to avoid the smoker was entirely subconscious. This behavior continued for many, many years and in some cases virtually the rest of their lives.

When fear, guilt, and worry are attached to sex it can be very difficult to separate them. This connection can be life long. It is little wonder that girls and women alike are not enjoying sex. Sex is a very powerful bonding tool and serves an extremely important purpose in marriage. If one, or both of the marriage partners associate sex with all that is bad, there is little hope of a fulfilling physical relationship. And yet we wonder why we suffer from a fifty percent divorce rate.

HORMONES-

"Hey, I am only human. Once my hormones get raging there ain't much I can do about it."

Hormones serve a normal, biological function. Hormones turn boys to men, and girls to women. They are good. They give us a sex drive and allow us to reproduce. So, in fact, the kids are right. Hormones do have a lot to do with why kids are going ahead and having sex before marriage. It can be a difficult, but not impossible, thing to overcome a hormonal drive.

The male hormone, testosterone, not only make guys extremely interested in girls, it also makes guys more aggressive. So not only are they interested they are more than likely going to pursue it with vigor. It is important to realize that a sex drive is real and it is normal. A sex drive is nothing to be ashamed or embarrassed about. The truth is however, that humans have all sorts of drives. Humans have a hunger drive. Humans have a thirst drive. All human drives are in place to ensure the survival of the species.

As humans though, we have learned to check our drives until the appropriate place and time. A high-school student gets hungry during the school day but rarely does he decide to start gnawing away on his tennis shoe. He waits for the right time, the lunch hour; and the right place, in the school cafeteria. Though when I use this analogy with the students some readily report that eating their own sneakers would be an improvement on the school cafeteria.

The sex drive too can, and should, be reserved for the right time and place. The right time could well be on their wedding night. The right place in this case, would be a honeymoon suite overlooking Niagara Falls. Sound corny? Sure it does, but it sounds a whole lot better than simply giving into one's hormonal urges in the back seat of your dad's Ford.

I like to tell girls that a man, a real man, should be in control of himself. If he cannot control his hormonal urges, he is unlikely to have control over other significant aspects of his life. This is a guy who is not a good bet for a long-term relationship.

Girls, on the other hand are not driven by testosterone. They are tanked up on estrogen. Estrogen does not give females an overly active sex drive and it does not make them aggressive. It gives them heightened emotions such as love and commitment. When their hormonally assisted desire for love and commitment meets up with a hormonally driven guy, we have both the opportunity for disaster or amazing success. The deciding issue is a matter of timing. Hormonal drives in a committed, monogamous relationship, serve as the glue that can help bond a couple together. Outside of this arrangement, we have the formula for a chemically fueled disaster.

LOVE -

"Love makes it alright, doesn't it?"

In almost every case 'love' as a reason to go ahead and have sex, is brought up by a girl. Only a couple of times in fifteen years of presenting, has this answer been bought up by a male student. It is not that the guys disagree with this answer; it is just that it is far from the top of their list.

I often tell the students that love is the real deal. That love really will protect them. If a young couple is in love, the girl will not experience an unplanned pregnancy. If a couple is in love, they will be protected from STDs. If they are in love, there is no chance of getting a bad reputation, and if your parents walk in on you, they just sigh and say, "It's okay, they're in love".

With each succeeding statement I try my best to sound more facetious than the sentence before. Almost everyone eventually catches on by the time I have completed my litany. However, once a girl who was an eighth grader at a local Catholic school was still hanging on my every word till the very end. Her classmate, sitting next to her noticed her rapt attentiveness and realized, as I had, that this girl actually believed me. A friendly slap to the back of her head and the words "He's kidding!" brought her back to earth.

The truth is, love really won't protect us against any of the risks of premarital sexual activity. In fact, love just might make it worse. Given the fact that only one-percent of high school couples ever become a long-term item, means there are bound to be a lot of broken hearts.

My day job work place offers counseling. Every year we get a significant number of females who are there because they were in a physical, intimate relationship that ended in a breakup. The fact that the girl gave not only her body, but her heart as well seems infinitely more damaging. Guys rarely seek out counseling for the same thing.

By and large, girls want love to be present before they get sexually involved. It really appears that most guys don't feel the same way. So how is it that so many girls, who want love in their relationship, are having sex with so many guys, who could care less about love? The answer is really quite simple. Guys lie. Not all guys and not about everything, but when it comes to sex, guys lie.

We are not afraid to ask the guys if they would be willing to lie in order to have sex with a girl. Most simply sit quietly. But with enough prodding, one-by-one they start to come clean. Of course, they admit, we will tell a girl what she wants to hear. But, according to them, it is not a selfishly motivated act. Many of them claim they lie so the girl will feel better about herself. You just have to love that sort of reasoning!

In any case, it seems that love is indeed a strong motivator for young women to consider engaging in a sexual relationship.

PROVE MANHOOD–

"There is a lot of guy-to-guy pressure. We gotta prove our manhood!"

Here is a newsflash that I share with students everyday. The ability to have sex does not prove you are a man. It proves you are a male. Male dogs have sex. Male rats have sex. Even male cockroaches have sex. Go out and have sex and all you have proved is that you are as good as a dog, a rat or a cockroach. Throw yourself a party!

The real news here is that self-control makes the man. Let me give a rather simple illustration. Imagine a two-year old boy. He is just minding his own business, when the doorbell rings. When mom answers the door, it is apparent to the two-year old that lots of company is coming. He gets very excited at the prospect of a lot of visitors. When finally the last of mom's six visitors arrive, she puts a fresh diaper on him and gives him a huge bottle full of apple juice with the hope that he will quietly drink his juice, allowing her to entertain her friends.

Of course, being a two-year old male, he has a different idea. He is going to make sure the ladies are entertained. So, he does his thing, running in circles, drinking his apple juice, while all the women giggle and enjoy his antics. At some point, the young boy tires and slows to a walk. It is at this point that he realizes that huge bottle of apple juice now has him on the verge of peeing his pants. He stops moving entirely, and is standing right in front of his mom and her friends. He is two. And he is wearing a diaper. What is he to do? Well, simply put. He is going to stand there, bend his knees slightly, look up to the sky, and pee. The big smile on his face is testament to his relief and that nice warm feeling in his pants. Every woman in that room knows exactly what he just did, but he does not care because he is two.

Now today, as a freshman in high school, you simply don't pee your pants. You use self-control. It is a sign of maturity. You wait for the right time and right place, between classes and in the men's room, to take care of such matters. Now every guy in the room is capable of peeing his pants. I suppose we could all line up side-by-side in the front of the classroom and on three could, in unison, pee our pants. But we would not do that, as maturity dictates otherwise. Just because we can do it, does not mean we would do it.

Sex is the same way. Just because we can do it, does not mean that we do. We are NOT like some monkey in a tree. We see a female monkey, hop down out of the tree, do our thing, and then climb back into the treetops. We are humans and we have the ability to exercise self-control. Self-control makes the man. Share this with every girl you know. If a guy cannot control his own urges what are his chances of controlling his education, his career, and his relationships with family and friends?

KEEP BOY/GIRL FRIEND-

"If you don't put out, and some other girl will, you can lose your boyfriend just like that!"

As you might suspect, there are many more girls who worry about keeping their boyfriend than there are boys worried about keeping a girlfriend. When in the classroom we do not diminish the possibility that young couples could be in love. We used to though. Just flat out told them they were too young to be in love. Well, if you ever want to know the quickest way to get a group of young people to ignore you, tell them they are incapable of falling in love.

We have actually had a good number of young men and ladies explain to us that they were in love and gave a pretty darned good definition of what makes a loving relationship. So, as of late, all of our classroom presentations acknowledge the prospect of love among the young. Before we get too far with this it is important to acknowledge that true love between teens is a very rare thing. There is plenty in the way of infatuation and lust to go around, but little in the way of love as we know it.

That aside, the prospects of a high school couple actually making it to the altar and becoming a married couple are about one in a hundred. This is not to say that people who attend high school together have a one-percent chance of getting married. It is to say that high school couples that profess to be in love have a one-percent chance of ever getting married to one another. One-percent. There is absolutely NO research that suggests that high school couples that have had sex together have any better chance of getting married. The odds for them are the same as for their non-sexually active high school peers.

I honestly believe there does not exist a girl who, expecting a perfect score on a recent test, would be happy with a one-percent. I wonder if any student, if promised one hundred dollars for raking leaves, would be thrilled to find out that the compensation had been reduced to one dollar. Yet young people, especially girls, will give themselves sexually in order to keep a boyfriend. They don't do this thinking they will have only a one-percent chance of keeping that boyfriend long term. They do it because they think they have a chance of keeping that boyfriend for a very long time.

Often, we hear of girls who will go so far as to intentionally get pregnant in order to keep a boyfriend that they fear they may lose. By hook or by crook they find a way, and before long they are pregnant. The real problem is that studies indicate that, in the event of a pregnancy, only three percent of the couples were actually still together after just two years. The study only lasted two years so there is no way of knowing what percentage of couples made it three, five, or even ten years. The really sad part is that the planned pregnancy can actually backfire and be the cause of the couple breaking up. The number one stressor in marriages today is money. Having a baby in high school will more than likely have a very negative financial impact. A young, high school aged couple is highly unlikely to be able to muster the resources needed to work things out. Ultimately, the stress will get the best of them and their relationship will be history.

ALREADY DID IT

"I have already had sex a bunch of times. Is there really any point in trying to stop now?"

Well of course there is. The risk is there with each and every sexual encounter. Reduce the number of sexual encounters, and you will undoubtedly reduce your risk of STDs, unplanned pregnancy and the other consequences that can come with premature sexual activity. There is no reason to believe that one must continue to engage in a risky or harmful behavior simply because they already have.

As an example of the foolishness of this kind of thinking I will act as though I have concluded for the day, whereupon I will head for the door. It is always closed, because I always close it as I begin my presentation. I will not reach for the knob and will try to simply walk through the door. Of course, I bang my forehead on the door (or so it seems) and bounce back into the classroom rubbing my noggin for all it is worth. Of course the students, being the loving and caring sort that they are, laugh their butts off.

So, as if they are not having enough fun at my expense, I repeat the exact same act. It may take one or two more tries, but eventually one of the kids will take pity on me and tell me that I need to turn the doorknob in order to open the door. If the kids do not play along I make sure the teacher gets me off the hook by providing me with this same information. It is at this point I launch into the point of this exercise. I can ignore the advice of the student and continue walking into that door until I knock myself silly. Or, I can take that student's advice and walk up to the door, turn the knob, and safely, without harm, exit the classroom.

It is very easy for the class to see that only a fool would ignore the advice of the student. I ask them though what is the point of following the student's advice? After all, I have already walked into the door a number of times. From there the connection is an easy one to make. They can readily see that there is no reason for a person to continue putting him or herself at risk, to continue hurting themselves. There actually can be good reasons to change one's behavior.

Even if a girl or guy has managed to avoid pregnancy and STDs, there is still the emotional impact of a past sex life. In girls particularly, the emotional impact can trigger a lowering of self esteem which can in turn lead to more bad decision making. Secondary virginity carries with it numerous benefits. It is important to convey to young men and women that changing from a life that is sexually promiscuous to one that is based on abstinence is something to be very proud of. Sex does feel good after all and doing a 180 and giving up sex must certainly be a difficult thing to do. Good for them if they can make such a good decision for themselves!

Always remember that past decisions make you who you are today; the decisions you make now and in the future will determine the person you will ultimately become.

REVENGE–

"If somebody steals my man and has sex with him, then I am going to steal hers and have sex with him. That is just the way it is."

This happens much more than any of us want to believe. Often times though, the girls seeking the revenge end up paying the biggest price of all. The girls end up pregnant or infected with an STD. Since their only motivation was revenge, they have little, if any, likelihood of developing a long-term relationship with their newfound sex partner. So they face the disease or the pregnancy on their own and doom themselves to a life with significantly more difficulties than their peers.

I don't even try to talk girls, who are hell bent on revenge out of getting revenge. I just suggest a much better plan. Long-term revenge. I ask them to imagine life one year after executing their plan of revenge. Pregnant, trying to raise a three month old on her own, or if she is lucky, with the help of her parents. All the while, the girl she was trying to get even with is making plans to go away to college. Some revenge huh?

I like my version better. Let the girl who 'stole' your boyfriend have him. Any guy that would cheat on you does not deserve you anyway. Now take all that energy you were planning to put into your revenge effort and use it to enhance your grades so you can get into a good college. There you will meet and eventually marry a premed student. Sometime after he has opened his very successful plastic surgery practice and you have completed your second year as the editor of a major fashion magazine, you will buy the biggest house in town. As things progress for you and your husband, you acquire all the fineries of life. You'll get a very nice swimming pool for the back yard. There will be a Porsche in the driveway for him and a Mustang convertible for you.

One day, just to pass the evening away you and your husband will be sitting on the gorgeous front porch of your house, where you enjoy a terrific view. While watching the occasional car pass in front of your house you notice a real beater heading your way. The only thing holding this car together is the rust. It is belching smoke like a fire breathing dragon. As the car cruises past your house, the female passenger looks your way, nearly gawking at the beautiful home and landscaped yard. You catch her eye and she catches yours. You realize you know her. Guess what? She is your old nemesis, the girl who stole your boyfriend. Judging by the completely different guy driving the car they are apparently no longer together.

You raise your hand to offer her a little wave hello and a smile. She meekly responds with one of her own. She continues driving on down the road in a car that may die at any moment. It is a safe bet, though, that the smile will not soon die from your face. Now THAT is revenge!

REBELLION–

"Sometimes you have to do something bad just to let your parents know that you are in charge of your life and they are not."

This is the one that my co-presenter Jen just loves to respond to. Perhaps it is because, deep down inside, she know this is one of the craziest of all the reasons we encounter. She tells it this way:

Imagine that you are sitting here in school and it is the day before the start of spring break. You and your friends have lots of plans for the nine straight days that you will be out of school. However, things change in a hurry as your overzealous math teacher, Mr. Poindexter, informs the class that he will be expecting a fifty page paper on the life of Albert Einstein on your first day back from the break.

Needless to say, you are ticked. You see this as ruining your entire spring break, and you are fuming mad. You are going to rebel. You are going to let Poindexter know just how ticked you are. You stand up right in the middle of class and walk to the front of the classroom. There you turn around and face the rear of the classroom. You place yourself directly in line with the widest aisle in the classroom. You choose the one that gives you the best and cleanest shot to the back of the room. At that point you put your head down and run as fast as you can into the cement block wall that is the back of the classroom.

Well in no time at all, you are flat on your back seeing stars in the middle of the day. Your head hurts like crazy and you now have one heck of a nosebleed. You have very successfully made your point. You have rebelled against the general order, and you have shown Mr. Poindexter that you are unhappy with him.

But who got hurt? Is your intended target hurting from this act of rebellion? Well, maybe. It is possible that he might just split a rib laughing his behind off at you, along with the rest of the class. But what have you really gained except the new class nickname "block head". It is a nice enough nickname but the outcome of your rebellious act has been anything but successful. You still have the paper to write and to make matters worse; you still have a heck of a headache.

Students are going to rebel. Some will rebel in small ways and some will make it a big time event. We let them know that if they are planning to make a really big statement that involves having sex with their current flame, that they would be better off sticking their hand in a blender. The point we try to make is, why hurt yourself to rebel. What sort of point are you really trying to make. Instead, why not dye your hair purple? Why not cut holes in all of your blue jeans. Something, anything, that will not result in permanent damage.

BORED–

"There is just nothing to do around here, so kids have sex just to kill the boredom."

On this, I absolutely have to agree with the students. There is no doubt in my mind that having sex will cure boredom. I mean let's face it, how boring do you think it is to have to get your best friend to buy a pregnancy test kit for you? How boring can it be to be a 14-year old girl just waiting to see the results of that pregnancy test? Does anyone really think it would be boring having to sit down and tell your mother, your father, and other members of your family that you are pregnant? Does any young man out there think it would be boring to have to tell your parents that your girlfriend is pregnant by your doing?

Could any young person be bored with the prospect of being tested for STDs? Better yet, should they find out they suffer from America's number one STD, HPV they might find themselves in need of treatment for genital warts. They are painful and unsightly and can be removed with a laser, a scalpel, or with liquid nitrogen. I don't know about you, but if someone were aiming a laser gun at a very private region of my body, I would be anything but bored. Beyond all this, there is always the chance of actually having a baby. Feeding and changing a baby every four hours, day after day and night after night. Finding a way to afford the diapers and formula that your baby will need will certainly not be boring. So young people, I agree, having sex will cure your boredom. However, you might want to consider joining the track team as a less permanent solution to your boredom.

TO FIT IN–

"In high school, even in middle school, fitting in is the most important thing on earth."

Ten years ago this was a very valid point, at least when it comes to high school students. A 1992 survey found that just over seventy percent of high school students were sexually active prior to graduation. Today, in 2005 this is no longer the case. Depending on the study, between fifty and fifty-four percent of high school students are now having sex prior to graduation. So we go from almost a fourth of students waiting, to nearly half of students waiting, and it is heading in the right direction.

So if a high school student, and certainly a middle school student, really want to 'fit in' they can be just as comfortable with the choice of abstinence.

One other problem with fitting in is that high school students, especially males, are known to greatly exaggerate their 'sexploits'. Guys could be sitting in the locker room after gym class listening to Tom brag about the latest notch in his belt. Not only does he brag about this latest conquest, he makes sure every guy within ear shot knows this is at least his tenth conquest. When he concludes his tale of conquest, he naturally looks to the next guy to share his stories with the guys. Bill, who is sitting right next to Tom takes up the mantle and tells his tales of romance and beyond. He might not have the quantity of girls that Tom did, but Bill makes sure everyone knows his girls were all about quality.

And so it goes around the locker room until it comes to you. Well, you know you are a virgin, but no one else in the room does. So you have a choice. You can stand up, stick out your chest and say "Not me fellas, I am a virgin!" Or you can lie. What do you think the average teenage male is going to do in a situation like that? You bet, he is going to lie. I really have no problem with the lie. In this case, if it saves you from total embarrassment, then I guess I can live with it. What worries me more is that the virgin student then walks out of the locker room under the delusion that every other guy in his entire gym class is sexually active. In his mind they are very sexually active.

It never occurs to this young man that he wasn't the only one fabricating his way out of a tough situation. If we can believe the national statistics, then about half the guys in the room were virgins right along with our fallen hero. More troubling though, is that he may act falsely on the information he perceives to be true. In an effort to fit in with the rest of the guys, he may seek to accelerate his personal timeline for the onset of sexual behavior. So it appears that 'fitting in' is not all it is cracked up to be, as a reason to have sex.

TO BE POPULAR-

"I would do anything to be more popular."

It is understandable that people want to be popular. What I cannot understand is their willingness to 'do anything' to gain that popularity. Girls especially, seem willing to throw caution to the wind. The tricky thing to convey here is that popularity for the person is a different thing than popularity for the body.

Say for example, that I went to the local high school every single school day. With me, I would bring more than enough candy bars for each and every student in that school. I would arrive before the students and set up in the main entryway. As the students entered, I would encourage them to help themselves to their choice of a candy bar.

I would come to that school day after day after day. Given enough time, I am confident that the students would enjoy a moment of conversation with me. Some would greet me with a simple "hello". Others might ask, "How are you doing?" Some would even spend some significant time chatting some of their morning away with me.

It would be easy for me to start feeling pretty good about myself. Here I am, a fifty one year old hanging with the high school kids. I might even go so far as to think of myself as cool. I assure you, I would have fun every single morning and I would enjoy the banter with the students. Eventually though, I would run out of money. Buying candy bars for 350 students a day can become a financial burden in very short order.

Of course, even though I was out of cash, I would continue going to the school every morning. I would have to. I would not want to let all my new friends down. Surely they would miss me. I imagine they would continue to greet me in the morning. Some would even continue to engage me in conversation. Why wouldn't they, after all I am popular.

Imagine though, that some new fellow starts showing up at the school every morning. He brings along his great big box of candy bars and sets up across the school lobby from me. He decides to give out free candy bars to the students as they enter the school every morning. In fairly short order the kids would quickly bypass my customary station and proceed directly to the new source of candy bars.

Oh sure, I might get an occasional hello, maybe even a full sentence worth of conversation. The truth is the new guy will, without doubt, appear to be exceedingly more popular than I am. I use the word appear for a reason. Was I ever really the popular one? How about the new guy, had he become more popular than me?

Well, in fact, neither of us was popular. Only the candy was. Girls who think they can be popular by giving away their sexuality will be shocked to learn that they have not become any more popular at all. Only their sex was. Of course guys will beat a path to the door of a girl who is willing to give her sexuality away. That line of guys is hollow victory for a girl wishing to be truly popular.

MEDIA PRESSURE-

"Sex looks just so awesome in the movies that I really can't wait to try it."

The media exerts a strong influence on our young people. In fact, the media exerts a strong influence on all of us. Without thinking too hard I want you to complete the following sayings for me:

"Just Do_____."

"Have it your _____."

"We love to see you _____."

Congratulations if you came up with "Just Do It," "Have it your way," and "We love to see you smile." Bonus points if you can name the companies represented by the above three slogans. Just in case you are in the 2% of our population that watches less than 30 minutes of television a day the answers are Nike, Burger King, and McDonald's. If you are anything like our students about 95 percent of you got a perfect six for six on the above quiz. This is not a quiz that anyone has to study for because the information is so imprinted on your brain that it is almost automatic. Of course, media includes more than television. Radio, movies, and print media all contribute to this saturation process. In any case the end result is that you just 'know' that at Burger King you can have it your way.

The average teenager sees 14,000 sexual encounters a year

on television. The vast majority of these are awesome, consequence free events that feature orchestra music, rose petals and fireworks. I have been married nearly 30 years. I think (hope) my wife would agree that we have a pretty darned good sex life. Sadly though, not once has orchestra music spontaneously begun playing in my bedroom. Not once have rose petals drifted down from the ceiling. I must admit that there was one time when fireworks started going off outside our bedroom window, but it turned out to be the Fourth of July, so I could take no credit for that!

Additionally, 14,000 sexual encounters seen per year portray a sexual activity rate that is totally unrealistic. Seeing that much sex on television alone would easily convince you that everyone is having sex all the time. This is so unrealistic. When I tell our students that the average married couple has sex twice a week they are in total disbelief. In his or her world, everyone (except their parents that is) is having sex every free moment.

The problem with the media becomes that, given enough exposures, people will automatically think sex is always awesome and prolific, and comes consequence free.
That perception can put a lot of pressure on a young person to get on the perceived bandwagon. It is up to parents to provide balance against what the media is portraying. Sadly, our numerous discussions with parents indicate that many of them are operating on the same page with their children!

Everyone needs to understand that the main purposes of media are to entertain and to sell. Neither of those necessarily requires that the truth be told.

POOR ROLE MODELS–

"My parents don't mind at all. In fact my mom put me on the pill when I was 12."

The kids are half right on this one. There are plenty of poor role models to go around. So many parents want to be their child's friend, that they have lost sight of their role as the person who sets the expectations for their children. In families where going to college is talked about as the normal course of events, the college enrollment rate is nearly double that of children from families who rarely discuss college.

Families that establish serious consequences for children who take up smoking, are much more likely to raise a life-long non-smoker. Parents can be the single most influential factor in their child's life. You have to know though that kids will do what you do, not what you say. Parents who wish to dissuade their children from smoking can impose all the consequences in the world but if the parents are smokers it will be a losing battle.

Parents have to know that they serve as models of behavior. Spouses who dally outside their marriage, single women who host the occasional overnight male guest, single men who entertain female visitors or spend the entire night out, are sending the wrong message to their children.

There was a long-standing myth that girls without fathers were much more likely to experience an unplanned pregnancy than their peers who had a father in the household.

In fact, some studies indicated that their risk was as much as seven times greater. Turns out however, that the studies were somewhat flawed. It was true that, as a group, the girls from fatherless homes were up to seven times more likely to experience a teen pregnancy. But within that statistic was an even more meaningful one. Girls who were being raised in a fatherless home and with a mother who entertained overnight male guests were up to thirty times more likely to experience a teen pregnancy. It also turns out that girls who came from fatherless homes who had a mother who absolutely never entertained overnight male guests, were no more likely to experience a teen pregnancy than their peers who had both a mother and a father in the home.

No matter what the parents did or did not do, the students were very adept at identifying which parental behavior was undesirable and which parental behavior was desirable. Kids who have parents who are involved in an affair were quick to identify that behavior as wrong and inappropriate. Students, who lived with single parents, knew it was wrong for mom or dad to have overnight guests. Kids know when their parents are setting a poor example when it comes to sexual behavior.

What is hard to understand is that even though they can identify the behavior as wrong or inappropriate, students with poor role models of parents are slightly more likely to engage in that behavior than their peers from households that exhibit appropriate behavior. So the 'poor role model' explanation for going ahead with sex is spot on, but only for a small percentage of students.

IMMUNE–

"I don't know anyone my age with an STD. I just don't think they affect young people."

We already know that young people are not immune from catching an STD. Sure, they are in the best shape of their lives. They can run all day and stay up all night. I like to tell them that as a high school student I could run a 4:54 mile. At the age of fifty-one I tell them I still can, only now it is four hours and fifty-four minutes. They do tend to think that "old folks" are the only ones who get sick. Another reason that most young people believe they are immune, is that they simply do not know anyone who is infected. Well, at least they think that is the case.

Remember our five rules of STDs. Rule number one was that you simply can't determine if someone has an STD. Because of this fact, a high school student surrounded by fellow students with STDs may not have the slightest idea that they were infected.

Another explanation for middle and high school students to believe they are immune from STDs is the gestation periods of STDs. While an infection, when caught, is caught immediately, the symptoms may take up to ten years to appear. Without symptoms, there is little reason for a person to even be tested for a disease. In a related matter many STDs are a symptomatic. They have no overt symptoms. In fact HPV, the leading STD, rarely exhibits symptoms in men at all.

Yet another explanation is likely due to the fact that those students who have been tested, and who are aware that they do indeed have an STD, are highly unlikely to publicize that fact. I think it is almost unimaginable that a guy would race through the halls of his high school, high fiving anyone in sight and screaming with joy that he just found out that he has syphilis! One final note, and in fact one of the saddest notes, is that not only are younger females not immune from STDs, they are in fact more susceptible to acquiring an STD than a girl in her twenties. The cervix is not fully formed in teenage girls. It is actually softer than it will be when a girl reaches her mid-twenties. This factor actually makes teenage girls more susceptible to an infection such as an STD.

CURIOSITY–

"I just want to see what it is like. Is there really any harm in that?"

Well yes, in fact there is. I think one of the hardest things to convey to young people is that you have to be on your best behavior all the time. Your child could lead a model life day after day, year after year. But, if they make just one bad decision, they could end up paying life long or life shortening consequences. It seems so unfair that a young person, who has led an exemplary life 99 percent of the time, could end up paying the same price as a kid who has been a foul-up his entire life.

The point is, that responding to curiosity could have very serious consequences. There is nothing wrong with curiosity in itself. Curiosity is a normal behavior. In fact, if your adolescent weren't curious about sex, I would be a bit concerned. But curiosity should not be so overwhelming that it cannot be controlled. Besides, the great thing about curiosity is that it will not go away. It will just get a little stronger as time passes. That growing curiosity just means that when the honeymoon finally rolls around there will be plenty of satisfaction to make the wait worth the while.

Let's take Christmas as an example. Imagine the average fifteen year-old boy. He has made it well known that he would like the latest version of the PlayStation for Christmas. He drops hints every chance he gets, proclaiming the 'total awesomeness' of the PS 10,000! So, parents being the loving types they tend to be, run out and secure a PS 10,000 for their son. They bring it home, wrap it in some suitable Christmas wrapping paper and hide it in the usual spot on the top shelf of the linen closet.

There on the shelf in the linen closet, the PS 10,000 sits unnoticed for at least the next four hours. Fifteen year-old boys being the curious sort are pretty much clued in to the hiding spots favored by their parents. So the very next time his parents leave the house, he runs to the linen closet and checks to see if there is anything hiding on that top shelf.

Lo and behold, there is a wonderfully wrapped package that is just about the right size and shape of that new PlayStation. The eager young fellow pulls it down off the shelf and gives it a little shake. Oh it definitely must be a PS 10,000. Just to make sure though, he slowly peels back the gift wrap just enough to reveal the label on the box. Unmitigated joy follows as the PS 10,000 logo comes into view. He is a very excited young man, and he would like nothing more than to play with his newfound treasure. It is not to be. His parents could return at any moment, so he knows he must restore the package to its original condition and get it tucked back safely on the top shelf.

His curiosity has been satisfied. But to what end? He really can't play with it. He can tell a couple of friends that he knows he is getting a PS 10,000 for Christmas but he can't tell everyone. He certainly would not want word getting back to mom and dad that he was a sneak. As the next six weeks pass, he waits patiently for Christmas morning when he will finally be able to open his prized Christmas present.

When Christmas day finally arrives, he sits with his older sister and baby brother opening the presents under the tree. They are obviously all excited by the presents, and mom and dad are just thrilled at the reaction the gifts are getting. Our young man opens his lesser presents, slowly working his way up to the big present. Of course, knowing what is already behind the wrapping paper, he realizes he will need to do a pretty convincing job of faking excitement for his parents. That he does. It is a masterful job of feigned joy. He has done his best acting job ever, and yet he knows it is not enough. He can tell by the look on his parents' faces that they know he was faking it. They know he peeked and he feels a little embarrassed by it.

Sex is the same way. Having it early makes it a sneaky venture. You can't really tell everyone, and you don't want your parents finding out. It really ruins it. When you get married sex becomes a very open thing. Not in the sense that it is done in the open, but in the sense that the fact that you are having sex is in the open. Not that kids need to come back from their honeymoon raving about all the fun they had having sex, but the fact is their parents know it and everyone is pretty much okay with it. I say pretty much everyone, because as the father of two girls, I really don't dwell much on the thought of my little girls having sex with their husbands, but I pretty much presume it is happening. In fact, I hope it is. Grandchildren are something I would like very much. The thought of future grandchildren born into a stable home life is about all a guy could ask for. It sure beats worrying about your daughter's premarital sex life and the ensuing consequences.

I apologize for straying off track there for a moment, but want to get back to the issue of curiosity. We share with the students that curiosity is normal. It is widely stated that the average teenage male thinks of sex every eight seconds. Having been a teenage boy, I can assure you that statistic is blatantly false. It is more like every four seconds. So long as the young man sticks to just thinking about it, all will be okay.

TO RELIEVE STRESS–

"Sex really does feel good and it really relaxes me."

This is another point at which we have to agree with the student's assessment. Sex can be very relaxing. Although I really wonder how relaxing sex can actually be for them. Let's face it; worrying about an unplanned pregnancy, acquiring an STD, earning a bad reputation, or getting caught in the act by your parents, cannot possibly be a stress reducer. In fact, I would think that quite the opposite would be true.

There is also the chance that any of those fears I have just mentioned could come true. An unplanned pregnancy is certain to be one of the greatest stressors anyone could ever experience. Just the thought of having to tell your parents something like that is enough to cause a sleepless night or two. Raising a child, even with your education complete and a supportive partner is stressful enough let alone trying to accomplish that as a single, undereducated parent.

Acquiring an STD, even a curable one, is still a stress-inducing situation. There are the tests needed to confirm and the appointments needed to get the treatment. There is the very invasive process of detailing your sex life and the joy of informing your past partners that they now may be infected with an STD. Relaxing? I think not. This does not even begin to describe the stress of acquiring an incurable STD.

Having a bad reputation, losing the trust of your parents, feeling guilt over a violation of your personal moral or religious beliefs, are all going to be stress inducers and not stress reducers.

This is not to say that young people do not have stressful lives. We really do not want to diminish their belief that they have stressful lives. They really do. Things are especially stressful in the areas of sex and sexuality. There is so much pressure on them to have sex that it is stressful in itself to decide to wait to have sex.

There are, of course, better outlets for dealing with stress. Getting involved in an after school activity that the young person truly loves (as opposed to one imposed by the parents) can be very effective. Schools sports and other extracurricular activities can have the same effect. Most of all however, understanding and compassionate parents who are there to listen to their children are perhaps the best bet of all.

MAKE BOYFRIEND HAPPY-

"I don't do it because he makes me, or because he would leave me. I just do it to make him happy. I really don't like having sex."

There is an old Diane Sawyer interview from a mid-90's edition of *Primetime Live* involving a group of 8th grade girls. Seeing this episode was one of the driving forces behind my involvement in the abstinence movement. Diane Sawyer spent the better part of the segment interviewing a group of three friends who spoke candidly about the prevalence of sex among their peers.

One of the girls had about ten partners, one had six or seven or eight (she really couldn't remember the exact number!), and one had three or four, depending on what was considered sex. They were so cavalier about it and proclaimed they were doing nothing unusual. That, in fact, they were better than most of their girl friends. They were asked about protection and all the girls acknowledged that they were not on the pill. They were asked specifically about condoms. One girl responded that, despite their ready availability at her school, she has never used condoms. Another offered that she and her boyfriends used condoms about half the time. And the final girl, the one who had "three or four partners", said she and her boyfriend did not use condoms, but when she had sex with other guys she always did.

As if all that was not shocking enough they were then asked why they got so heavily into sex at such a young age.

All three of the girls stated they were just doing what everybody else was doing. One of the girls took it a little further and explained that she does not even like having sex. Diane Sawyer seemed amazed by that revelation and asked her to clarify her comments. They really did not need much in the way of clarification and she simply restated that she did not like having sex. When asked why she kept on having it, she answered that she did it to make her boyfriend happy.

This is the statement that really bothered me. It was odd too because in marriage the concept of making sacrifices to keep the other partner happy can be a pretty noble concept, especially if the favor is returned in kind, at some future point. At the age of fourteen though, it seemed very sad. Here was a very beautiful young lady with her whole life ahead of her, who did not like having sex. Despite that, she continued having sex anyway. What chance do you suppose she will ever have of having the normal, enjoyable sex life we each deserve?

As a concluding question, the girls were asked what they would do if they had a chance to do it all over again. Every girl on the show, there were a total of seven of them, replied that they wish they had never started. They all wished they had waited until they were married. When asked why they just didn't stop and start life over again, one of the girls responded it was hard because guys just expected her to go all the way.

How sad. Sex should be a mutually rewarding experience. Sex was not designed to be endured by one partner to the exclusive benefit of the other.

DRUGS / ALCOHOL –

"I am just no fun at parties unless I have a couple of beers. If that means I get taken advantage of – then, oh well."

Seventy percent of high school aged girls who lose their virginity report that alcohol was involved. The vast majority of these girls wish they had never given up their virginity at that encounter. The alcohol lowered their resistance and also lowered their decision-making capacity. You have likely seen the proliferation of spring break videos displaying all sorts of unseemly, alcohol fueled, behavior. That nonsense that you see on those videos is behavior they know is being recorded. Imagine what goes on when they are operating under the assumption of privacy. On second thought, you may not want to imagine that.

Guys too, can suffer the effects of alcohol and drugs. Guys, who tend to have less in the way of inhibitions than girls to begin with, only exacerbate the problem with alcohol consumption. Once they get their 'beer goggles' on every girl starts looking pretty good. A guy could, and has, easily gotten a girl pregnant that he does not even know. Imagine the joy of delivering that child support payment on a monthly basis, to a virtual stranger!

The solution here is so simple it boggles the mind. Don't drink. We know that young people experience a lot of peer pressure in this area as well. For those kids unwilling to take a stand, I have some advice. If you really feel the overwhelming need to fit in at a party where there is a lot of drinking taking place, then grab that one can of beer and carry it with you all night long. No one there will know if that is your first beer or your second or your tenth for that matter. Better to be a little deceptive, than to pay child support for the next eighteen years.

One complicating factor in this area is the excessive amount of parental support for teen age drinking. I have more than a few relatives who think it is just hilarious when their high school aged children get drunk. It is a real laugh riot. I haven't the time or space here to go into all the health and risk factors that go along with that sort of behavior. Suffice it to say, that in the area of sex, it can lead to all sorts of bad decisions.

EVERYBODY IS DOING IT-

"I absolutely do NOT want to be the last person in my class who has sex."

Let me make this simple. Everyone is not doing it. Despite what they hear on the radio, see on the television or read in the tabloids, only about half of America's high school students are 'doing it'. While that number might be discouraging to some, for us in the abstinence business it is quite refreshing news. Less than fifteen years ago the number of high school students engaged in sexual activity was much closer to three-fourths!

This statistical change is testimony to the fact that young people are a whole lot more than the out of control, sex crazed animals that the pro-condom crowd would have you believe they are. In fact, they are quite capable of making a good and healthy decision for themselves. Our government, with the introduction of comprehensive sex education into our schools in the sixties, was pretty much saying exactly the same thing.

Here is a newsflash to all the individuals, groups, and agencies who have so little faith in our young people that you think the only solution is to strap a condom on them or put them on a daily pill. Young people are not animals. The folks who believe in abstinence only education believe in young people. We have faith that they will gather the facts and make good decisions.

What's Love Got To Do With It?

I mentioned a little earlier that 'love' only made the list of reasons to go ahead. Nearly every class we have presented to over the past fifteen years has listed love among the top ten or so reasons to go ahead with sex. In the vast majority of these cases, it was a girl who brought the item to the list. Just five or six times over the years has a guy listed love as the reason to go ahead.

Rarer still is the number of times anyone ever lists 'love' as a reason to wait. Sure, once in a while a very rare kid comes along and lists 'love' on "the reason to wait" list, but this is a very rare occurrence. I must admit that this perplexes us. Furthermore, we can think of no better reason to delay the onset of sexual activity than the fact that you love someone.

Love, to me, means that you care about the other person more than you care about yourself. Why would any young man who professes to be in love with a girl, expose her to the risk of an unplanned pregnancy, an STD, gaining a bad reputation, feeling guilty about violating her religious or moral beliefs, disappointing her parents and a host of other difficulties.

Why would any young woman who professes her love of her boyfriend, put him at risk for twenty years of child support, acquiring an STD, guilt over violation of moral or religious beliefs, and the interruption of his educational and career goals.

This does not sound like love to me. It sounds selfish to the point of ridiculous. It seems hard to imagine that a guy would put his girlfriend at such risk over a few moments of his own physical pleasure.

Even if a kid were selfish by nature, I can still make a pretty good case for delaying the onset of sexual activity until married. I would want my future wife to be all she can be before we took the chance of starting a family. I would want her to get all the education that she wants. I would encourage her to pursue her career dreams. The reason? Her success would be my success. For the selfish among us this means that, with my wife as a top-notch doctor, I will have the house, the car, and the fishing boat of my dreams.

Imagine a world where the girls and the guy each want their partner to be all they can be before they marry and before they begin their sex lives. Both individuals have obtained high level degrees and both are professionally very successful. All kidding about selfishness aside, imagine the lifestyle you, your spouse and your children would experience. Imagine the improvement of that life style over one that is forced into underachievement by an unplanned pregnancy.

We ask young people who believe they are in a loving and sexual relationship to put that relationship to the test. We ask them to tell their partner what they have learned in the classroom and then to explain further, that they have decided to terminate the sexual side of their relationship until they are married. If your partner really cares about you he or she will hang in there with you. If your partner was there just for the sex, then you can pretty much count on them breaking the relationship off. In the end, that would be good news. The sooner a person finds out that their partner was only sticking around for the sex, the better. While I don't doubt that a breakup could be emotionally difficult it would seem a better way to go than a breakup following an unintended pregnancy.

We nearly always run into high school couples that claim they know they are going to get married. They claim to be monogamous and they wonder why it is not okay for them to start the sexual side of their relationship right now. We have already discussed the importance of taking the time to establish the proper foundation for a relationship before it becomes sexual, but beyond that I believe that giving into sexual urges is a sign that the couple really does not believe they will make it as a couple.

If a couple truly believes they are going to be married then why the rush to have sex? Why not let each other achieve all that will be needed to ensure a more solid and comfortable marriage? It is simple, if a couple really believes they are going to get married, then they know they can wait to get started. They know all the sex they will ever want awaits them, and it comes without the consequences associated with premarital sex.

Let's face it. The list of "reasons to wait" suddenly becomes moot. Pregnancy is generally welcomed in marriage and not only by the parents, but by the grandparents and other family members as well. If both people waited for marriage to have sex, neither will bring an STD into their marriage and they can have all the sex they want without fear of acquiring an STD. By waiting they will have completed their education and will have started their career. Most likely, they will have honored their religious and moral beliefs. The reputation you earn by waiting until your wedding day is good one and actually earns you the right to wear white on your wedding day.

You will be able to safely and securely satisfy your curiosity and you won't have to keep it a secret. Your hormones will get the chance to do their thing, and you will be pleasantly surprised to see that they did not desert you when you decided to put off making use of them.

Are you noticing how all the things on that "why wait" list just vanish when you wait until you are married to begin your sex life? It all seems so simple, almost too good to be true. But it is not. And this is the good news that we need to share with our children, which leads me to the next chapter.

Where Do Parents Fit In?

We have had the opportunity to do a lot of research in the preparation of this book. Some of what we have learned has been alarming, some disturbing, and every once in a while we come across a great piece of news. The great news here is that parents are the single most influential force in their children's lives. Before we all leap for joy I do need to temper that news just a bit. There are exceptions to the rule. However, I still find this to be very encouraging. You may be wondering why, if this is really the case, if parents really are so influential, do we have runaway STD rates among our teens? And why are there a million unplanned teen pregnancies every year? Why do approximately half the teens in America decide to have sex while still a high school student? The answer is really quite simple. Parents may not know they have this influence or they simply are not making use of it. Worse yet is the possibility that parents just don't care if their kids are sexually active at an early age.

Since you are reading this book I will assume you do care. As such, it is imperative that you let your children know what the expectations are. The federal government in awarding abstinence education dollars expects us to convey the message that "abstinence from sexually activity until marriage is the expected standard of human behavior". At the very least this is the same standard that YOU need to set for your children. Your children want to please you and they want to measure up to the standards you set for them. Can you imagine how difficult it must be for a child to live up to standards that have never been set? Tell your child that you expect them to save sex for marriage.

Tell them they deserve a great sex life and this is the best possible way to achieve it.

Parents have expressed to me the great difficulty this task presents them. A lot of parents just don't know where to begin. When and how to set these expectations? What is the right age? How much is too much? Should there be other expectations set? To illustrate how difficult this can be for some parents let me once again share the story of the father of an eighth grade girl who recently attended one of our parent presentations. Our presentation is basically a summary of everything you have read in this book. We tell parents they need to get involved and explain the need to set expectations for their children. We discuss the value of being open and available to future questions they may have. The father, who by his presence showed himself to be a concerned parent, asked when was the right time to have "the talk" with his daughter. I, assuming he was referring to a younger daughter at home, asked him how old his daughter was. He looked a bit mystified by my question and answered that she was fourteen. I told him the right time for "the talk" with his daughter was about ten years ago.

In reality, "the talk" is a bit of a misnomer and should not be considered a single event. Think of it as more of a process, one that should start about the time toilet training starts. This is the time they will start to notice that they have special parts for special functions. They will be ready to learn a little more about their body every day. Just enough information is given so as to not be confusing or overwhelming. The key is that the child needs to have all the facts of life by the time they reach puberty. After this the talk can start to get a little awkward. Awkward as it might be, you need to maintain an ongoing dialogue. You will need to create a life long environment where your children will know that they can come to you any time they have a question about this or any other matter.

Along with the facts come the expectations. Your explanation that sex is for married couples to have babies can go a long way to setting up a lasting notion in your child's head. Don't be afraid to tell your child that you would be disappointed if they ever had to drop out of school. If you want them to attend college then start talking about it now and talk about it often. If you want your child to get good grades tell them that, and then set up an environment that will help them get there. It is all about expectations. Don't be afraid to share them with your child but be careful not to get carried away. Expectations need to be achievable and they need to be structured so a child can succeed on a one-day-at-a-time basis. You will need to tell your children what they need to know, instead of what they want to hear. You will want to set rules that will serve to be supportive of your expectations; rules on dating, rules on curfew, rules on the use of the computer, the phone, and the television. Rules will typically support more than one expectation. A "no television in the bedroom" rule can contribute to reduced negative influences, more family times and more time to keep up with studies.

If you hope to raise a child of virtue, you will have to do your part to create a supportive environment. Here are a couple of rules that are statistically supported by research and historic outcomes. Again, there are always exceptions to every rule, so these might need a little fine-tuning.

No opposite sex visitors to the bedroom, ever! The bedroom is for sleeping and dressing and undressing. Do you really want your child to intermingle those functions with members of the opposite sex?

No television in the children's bedroom. This can be adjusted at a later age, but the influence of media can be very negative. As such, it is best that a family watch television together. That way, you will see what they see and you will be there to clarify information for them.

All access to the Internet must be monitored. Much the same argument as for the television applies here. In addition the Internet is rife with pornography and predators. Put the computer in a very visible place and let your children know that there are no secrets when it comes to the computer. Friends of mine, Bill and Kay Malloy, installed a video monitor in their kitchen. It was linked to their son's computer. He was fully aware that his computer activity was under constant watch.

Telephones. Telephones. Telephones. This was once much easier to police and control. Now it seems everyone has a cell phone. This likely brings with it more good than bad. This does not mean there should not be rules. Most revolve around issues of common sense and courtesy. No using the phone at the movies or in a restaurant. Calls are not taken during the dinner hour. No long conversation when they have a guest. You get the idea.

Clothing is NOT optional. To clothe means to cover. Moms, I know you think you daughter is the hottest thing since sliced bread, but I (and the several thousand teen boys in your part of the country) do NOT need to see her belly, her butt, or her breasts! You and she may think it is cute but guys think it is a come on. In addition stop dressing your nine-year old like she is nineteen! The world has already been sexualized enough!

NO DATING until the age of sixteen (at the earliest). A girl who begins dating at the age of 15 is twice as likely to experience an unplanned pregnancy than does a girl who begins dating at 16. A 14-year old is nearly six times more likely to experience an unplanned pregnancy than her 16-year old counterpart. The numbers just keep getting worse as the girls get younger. Conversely, if you want to make a real impact, a girl who does not begin dating until age 17 is half as likely to experience an unplanned pregnancy as a 16-year old. If your daughter can manage to delay the start of dating until the age of 18, she is one-sixth as likely to experience an unplanned pregnancy as a 16-year old.

Curfews need not be an issue of contention. You have to be smart here. If you have done a good job of raising responsible kids, I recommend a strategy that worked well for me. As high school students, my son and two daughters had no curfew. This was a privilege earned by their behavior up to that point in their lives. They knew that privilege was theirs as long as they did not abuse it. They never did. In fact, they were home earlier than most of their friends and certainly earlier than I would have set their curfews for. You see, they were able to tell their friends they did not have a curfew, which gave them all the 'cool' they needed. Since the time to return home was their choice, there was no friction in our household over the issue of curfews. Of course, if your child has some problems in the area of responsibility, you will need to exercise more control in this area. Just in case you are wondering, I can't imagine an instance where a high school student would need a curfew any later than 11:00 PM on school nights and midnight on weekends. Sound too strict? Spend one month reading the crime and accident reports for your community and you too will be convinced.

Setting all the rules and expectations in the world will do you no good if you do not walk the walk! Kids will do what you do way before they will do what you say. It is your responsibility to be a good role model. Even the very little things can add up. One Sunday afternoon I had my laptop set up on the ottoman in front of me. On either side of my computer were stacks of notes for this book. I was leafing through the stacks seeking the information I needed to finish this chapter. My 18-month old grandson, Dominic, walked over and stood beside my ottoman and watched me type. He just stood there quietly. His only movement was that he kept putting his index finger on the tip of his tongue and then on my stack of paper. I watched him and wondered just what the heck he was doing. I was perplexed. Until, that is, I realized I was wetting my fingertip to make flipping the pages an easier task. He hadn't been watching me for more than a minute and he was already imitating my behavior. He is just 18-months old. Imagine what a kid will imitate when he is a bit older and when he is exposed to the behavior for more than a minute or so. It is up to you to model the sort of behavior today that you want from your child in the future.

The Case For Abstinence Education

STDs, unplanned pregnancy, emotional damage, physical consequences, and social and financial damage are all reasons in themselves for abstinence until marriage. One thing that is often overlooked however is the toll premarital sexual activity can have on your future relationships. Sex can be a powerful attractant. Young people, who choose to jump to the sex part of a relationship, sadly miss out on the relationship building that should occur prior to sex.

If a person wants to build a really solid house, they start with a lot of ground preparation. Then a footer of solid concrete is poured around the entire perimeter of the future house. The footer must be placed with care, and has to be perfectly level in order to be 100 percent effective and safe. Once the footer has had time to cure properly, a foundation wall of either concrete block or solid concrete is constructed atop it. At this point, floor joists of a carefully predetermined size are set atop the foundation wall and carefully secured according to the legal requirement of the local building code. Once the floor joists have been set, the entire surface is sheathed with plywood or OSB. From there the wall systems are erected into place to be topped by the roof trusses. Roof trusses are complex arrangements of timber and fasteners, computer designed to safely span the space below, while providing load carrying capacity of the sheathing, shingles and any potential snow load. When all that is finally in place, the roof sheathing can be affixed to the trusses, after which the shingles can be affixed.

Have you ever seen anyone start the construction of a house

by doing the shingling first? The roof system does not go up before the walls. And if walls are built without a proper foundation atop a proper footing, the house will collapse in short order.

Sex in a relationship is the LAST step. It is the roof on the house. Relationships too, need a solid footing in order to survive over the long haul. I always ask the students to give me their guess as to the average number of times a married couple has sex in a given week. I usually get two answers, one answer for their parents, and another answer for all other married adults. Most kids, jokingly I think, claim their parents do not have sex. When it comes to the rest of the married population the guesses always start optimistically high. Fifteen. Twelve. Nine. The guesses keep coming and I keep giving a 'thumbs down' sign. Finally, they arrive at the magic number of two. That's right. The average married couple in America has sex twice a week. The average amount of time spent in each sexual encounter is just under 20 minutes each.

So there you have it, the average married couple in America has sex for about forty minutes a week. Sex is indeed a powerful attractant, but it is NOT enough to carry a relationship on just forty minutes a week. If a couple has not invested the time to build a solid foundation for their relationship what is it they expect to do the other 6 days, 23 hours and 20 minutes per week. Yet, we continue to be alarmed by a 50 percent divorce rate. A young couple that jumps right into sex might well mistake physical chemistry for love. Of course, being young they are likely having sex much more often that the average of twice per week. Sex is their entire relationship. If they marry at this point there is little likelihood of long-term success. Once the sex slows down, and it always does, they find they really have nothing else in common.

Despite all of this common sense and logic, there are those who dismiss abstinence education out of hand. I am continually amazed when I hear folks say that abstinence won't or doesn't work. Of course abstinence works. Abstaining from sexual activity is, in fact, the only one hundred percent certain way to avoid pregnancy and STDs.

I think what they really mean is that students will not choose to follow abstinence. Certain high profile people make a point of attacking abstinence education programs. What is interesting is that when abstinence programs were initially funded, there was barely a ripple. After all, comprehensive sex education programs have been reaping government funding for nearly half a century.

It seems the onslaught against abstinence education started picking up steam at about the same time that abstinence education was proving to be effective. Some very strong special interest groups had a lot of money to lose if the abstinence movement were allowed to continue gaining acceptance. Condom and other contraceptive producers, drug companies, and abortion providers, for example, all stand to lose a lot of income. Sometimes it is easy to think that their objections to abstinence education are driven solely by money. Perish the thought.

As if this is not bad enough, they pass off their desire for abstinence education to be a flop as if it is an established fact. While I could respond to their false claims, I think it best to hear it in the words of Joe S. McIlhaney, MD, and the Director of the Medical Institute for Sexual Health.

What follows is the exact text of a letter written in December of 2004 to the Washington Post by Joe S. McIlhaney, MD and the Executive Director of the Medical Institute for Sexual Health.

To the Editor,

Representative Henry Waxman's critique of abstinence-education curricula is filled with misstatements, thus shedding more darkness than light on how best to help young people avoid the risks of sexual activity.

Contrary to your story (which criticized the effectiveness of abstinence education), there is considerable research documenting that abstinence-education programs produce measurable benefits. For example, a public school abstinence-education program in Monroe County, NY proved successful in both lowering sexual activity among 15-year-olds and pregnancy rates among girls ages 15 through 17. A recent study of teenagers who sign virginity pledges found that they are less likely to have sex in high school or to ever parent a child out-of-wedlock than their counterparts. And an abstinence program developed by Grady Memorial Hospital in Atlanta, according to a study published in Family Planning Perspectives, reduced the onset of sexual activity during the 8th grade by some 60 percent for boys and over 95 percent for girls.

Are there some mistakes in some of the curriculum used by abstinence-educators, including materials we have pro-

duced? Yes, as with all curriculum. Had Congressman Waxman shined an equally bright light on the traditional, so-called comprehensive sex education programs, he undoubtedly would have found as many if not more mistakes. For example, a publication issued by the Sexuality Information and Education Council of the United States (SIECUS) has stated that condoms are 98 percent effective in preventing pregnancy when used correctly and consistently (something teenagers rarely do) – this has only been shown to be true in one study of women over 35 who used condoms for at least four years. (SIECUS apparently felt that the volumes of research showing much lower effectiveness rates were not worth quoting – author's commentary)

Pointing out mistakes in curricula provides no insight into how best to help America's young people. Looking at results does. Not a single school-based "comprehensive sex-ed" program has been shown to lower STD, HIV, or non-marital pregnancy rates. The only so-called comprehensive sex-ed program ever to document decreased pregnancy rates did so by injecting young people with Depo Prevera, and this program has never published their STD rates. Abstinence-education, on the other hand, a relatively young field, is delivering positive results, which is why, in a recent Zogby poll an overwhelming majority – 85 percent – of parents said that the emphasis placed on abstinence for teens should be equal to or greater than the emphasis placed on contraception.

Sincerely,
Joe S. McIlhaney
The Medical Institute for Sexual Health

For me, it boils down to a couple of points of contention. The anti-abstinence crowd likes to claim that abstinence education won't work because kids are going to go ahead anyway and have sex. Therefore, we need a more "comprehensive" approach. While that might initially strike you as valid, it tends to strike me as insulting. What exactly are they saying about our young people? That they are incapable of making a healthy choice for themselves? That they are like some mindless animal that simply must give it to its sexual urges? That parents have absolutely no impact on the future decision making of their children?

I don't believe any of that. I see proof every single day that young people CAN make good decisions. I see that they are not slaves to their hormones. I see the amazing effect that strong and encouraging parents can have on their children.

I am pretty much fed up with social workers, teachers, counselors, medical professionals, politicians, and others whose sole claim to the need for comprehensive sexual education is that young people are "going to do it anyway" so we should at least teach them how to protect themselves.'

I have two arguments with that point:

   1) Does the belief that kids will "do it anyway" mean we should give up on them. For example, if a medical professional were counseling a suicidal patient, at what point would that professional give up and say " I know you are going to go ahead and do it

anyway, so here are some drugs that will make it as quick and as pain free as possible." I would hope that would never happen.

2) At best, comprehensive sexual education can offer only limited protection against some STDs.

Here is the bottom line. Those who advocate for comprehensive sexual education are putting children, your children at risk. If a young person decides to follow the comprehensive route, they still face the prospect of acquiring an STD or experiencing an unplanned pregnancy. Those who advocate abstinence education are not putting your children at risk. If a young person decides to follow the abstinence route, they will remain disease and pregnancy free. Oh, and by the way, when young people choose to follow the concepts presented in comprehensive sexual education lots of companies make lots of money. When a young person chooses to practice abstinence he, his family and society in general are the beneficiaries.

The Case Against Condoms

The point has already been made that condoms are not synonymous with safe sex. However, there are certain elements in our society that would have you believe that condoms are the be all and end all of a protected sex experience. Condom manufacturers, who benefit from the sale of condoms, and Planned Parenthood, who benefits from the failure of the condoms they recommend, heavily promote condoms.

In 2002, The Medical Institute for Sexual Health released Sex, Condoms, and STDs: What We Now Know. The report reviewed the findings of all significant research about the condom's ability to lower the risk of acquiring an STD.

Some of the key findings of their report, taken directly from their press release of October 16, 2002 are as follows:

- Even 100 percent condom use does not eliminate the risk of any STD including HIV.
- One hundred percent use of condoms for many years is so uncommon that it is almost a purely theoretical concept except for very few, very meticulous individuals. Even among adults who knew that their partner had HIV, only 56 percent used condoms every time.
- There is no evidence of any risk reduction for sexual transmission of human papilloma virus infection (HPV) even with 100 percent condom use.

- Syphilis transmission is reduced from 29 to 50-percent with 100 percent condom use, leaving a 50 to 71 percent relative risk of infection.
- Gonorrhea transmission is reduced approximately 50 percent with 100 percent condom, use leaving an approximate 50 percent relative risk of infection.
- Chlamydia transmission is reduced by approximately 50 percent with 100 percent condom use, still leaving an approximate 50 percent risk of becoming infected with Chlamydia.
- A recent study showed that with 25 percent or more condom use, the risk of transmission of genital herpes is reduced for females but not for males. Expanded data by the same author, as yet unpublished but presented at a national STD conference, shows risk reduction of approximately 40 percent for both males and females when condoms were used for 65 percent or more of sex acts leaving approximately a 60 percent relative risk of infection.
- HIV sexual transmission is reduced by approximately 85 percent with 100 percent condom use leaving an approximate 15 percent relative risk of infection with this usually fatal disease.
- For the approximately twenty other STDs, not enough data exist to say whether or not condoms offer any risk reduction from sexual transmission.

If the above information is unconvincing because it appears to stand alone in the face of all the positive promotion given to condom use in the past then read on. What follows, are the findings from a National Institutes for Health (NIH) report on the scientific evidence on condom effectiveness for sexually transmitted disease (STD) prevention. The report finding found, in their exact words:

- Consistent condom use reduces the yearly risk of contracting HIV from an infected sexual partner via vaginal sex by approximately 87 percent.
- Consistent condom use also reduces the risk of gonorrhea transmission from women to men.
- Consistent condom use may or may not reduce the risk of chlamydia transmission from women to men.
- Consistent condom use does not appear to reduce the risk of transmission of human papilloma virus (HPV) infection from men to women. Some evidence exists that condoms may reduce the risk of genital warts.
- There was insufficient data to make statements about condom effectiveness for any other STDs, including gonorrhea or chlamydia transmission from men to women and transmission of genital herpes, trichomoniasis, chancroid or syphilis.

So there you have it. Condoms, if used correctly and used 100 percent of the time, can reduce the risk of catching some STDs like HIV. Condoms, even if used correctly and used 100 percent of the time, cannot assure 100 percent protection against ANY STD. Condoms, even if used correctly and used 100 percent of the time, do NOT appear to reduce the risk of an HPV transmission.

HPV is the leading STD in America. It is little wonder, given that the latest research indicates there is no effective way of having sex and protecting against the transmission of HPV. HPV leads to nearly 100% of all cervical cancer cases. Many more women will die of cervical cancer this year than from HIV/AIDS. Yet many groups, even groups who include women's rights among their listed purpose for existence, continue to tout the value of condoms. I am at a loss to explain why so many individuals, groups, and organizations are willing to sacrifice so many women to cervical cancer, in the name of sexual freedom.

The Centers for Disease Control (CDC) in Atlanta notes that the surest way to eliminate risk for genital HPV infection is to refrain from any genital contact with another individual. For those who choose to be sexually active, a long-term, mutually monogamous relationship (we call this marriage) with an uninfected partner is the strategy most likely to prevent genital HPV infections.

As important as the STD issue is, the case against condoms extends well beyond that solitary issue.

Condoms, even if used correctly, are not 100 percent effective in eliminating the chance of pregnancy. The television show *Friends* was pretty much the poster child for promiscuous behavior. However, there was one memorable episode that pretty much said it all when it comes to condoms and pregnancy prevention. It was the episode where Ross inadvertently got Rachel pregnant. She broke the news to him as gently as possible, but as you can imagine he flipped out.

"But we used a condom", were the first words out of his mouth. Rachel replied by telling him that condoms fail sometimes. Ross, still in shock insists "they should put that on the label!" Rachel, still as calm as can be, tells Ross that they do put that on the label. Ross runs from the living room to the bathroom and back to the living room, where he is shown squinting at a condom package. Finally, after a great deal of scrutinizing he says "They should print it bigger!"

Ross is right; they really should print it bigger. They should also print that condoms are ineffective against a number of STDs.

In addition to STDs and pregnancy, condoms are useless when it comes to protecting your heart or your emotional well-being. Condoms do not protect your reputation. Condoms will do nothing to relieve the guilt over violating your personal religious beliefs. Condoms will not protect you against the hurt that your parents or other family members will feel when they find out you are pregnant or infected. Telling them you used a condom won't be of much comfort.

Some time ago, someone decided that condoms were a good substitute for self-control. It is really quite apparent that this grand experiment has failed. And it has failed miserably.

NOTICE!

The following chapter is not an endorsement of religion. It is an exploration of the subject for those students, parents and educators who operate under the impression that religion does matter.

Reading this chapter in a public school setting could result in your suspension, expulsion, or termination!

Proceed at your own risk.

This cost of printing this chapter of the book was paid with a private donation. The cover price has been adjusted downward to reflect this savings.

Where Does God Fit It?

This one is easy. God invented sex, so He fits in just fine. When we find ourselves presenting in a faith-based school where we are allowed to address matters of faith we revel in the fact that sex is inherently good because God invented it. That is a very strong endorsement!

Of course, I have taken a few creative liberties when telling the story of the day God invented sex for us.

It was just at the conclusion of the story of the creation. God was looking down, surrounded by His angels, admiring a job well done. The angels too, were all rather impressed and there was plenty of back slapping to go around that day in heaven. After a while though, God starts to shake his head ever so slowly. The angels immediately knew that God was a little displeased about something. One gathered the nerve to ask what was troubling the Lord.

He responded, "Something is missing. I love what I have done and man stands above all creatures as my favorite." The angels gathered closer as God continued. "But something is missing. I want to do something extra special for man and I just don't know what it should be."

One of the angels, a fairly outspoken one at that, suggested that God let man share in one of His miracles. God thought for just a moment, beamed a huge smile, and was obviously pleased. "That is a wonderful idea", God responded. "But I wonder which miracle it should be?"

"Perhaps" offered one of the angels "you could let them turn water to wine." At first, it appeared as though God was pleased, really pleased with that idea. But upon reflection He thought better of it and said. "I like the idea, but you know those kids at the Catholic schools. Every time they walk past a school fountain they'll be all like making the sign of the cross and WHOOSH! no more water fountain. Just the finest merlot ever known."

The angels continued to suggest miracles for God to bestow upon man.

"How about the walking on water thing?" intoned one. "No," God replied, "walking on water is only cool if you are the only one who can do it. Besides I have made man smart enough to invent boats, so they won't even need to be able to walk on water."

"I know," said another angel, "maybe you can let them raise people from the dead." God pondered a moment and responded, "Well, I don't think so. For one thing I am looking forward to man joining me here in heaven upon his passing. For another, things will get too crowded down there. Everybody will just keep bringing everybody back to life. It'll just be a big mess."

The angels were on the verge of giving up when a normally shy one asked if God would consider letting them create life. God was instantly pleased. He loved the idea. "That's it" God replied with a smile. "That is my very best miracle of all. It is the perfect one for man. I will let them create life. It will be so incredible. Not only that" continued God, "but I am going to make it an amazing experience. It will be fun. It will be loving. I will make man a female partner and together they will share this miracle."

The angels sighed. Perhaps they were even a little bit jealous. I mean God was making such a fuss over man. One even decided to play devil's advocate (if you will).
"Lord," he asked rather timidly, "aren't you worried that you might make it too much fun. That people will just do it to do it?" God thought long and hard. He had the answer "I see your point. Worry not, I will send down a very explicit instruction manual. It will make very clear that this creating life miracle (we call it sex) will be reserved for marriage. It will be known that it is not for mere entertainment. That way, there will be no problems. After all I am quite sure that man will be an obedient servant".

This instruction book that God sent our way, whether it be in the form of the Bible, the Torah, or the Quoran, is very clear on the fact that sex is reserved for marriage. It seems we have gotten ourselves into the fix we are in because we aren't quite the obedient servants that God had hoped we would be.

Every positive thing that sex can be gets all messed up when sex occurs outside of marriage. He has designed it to be awesome in so many ways; physical, emotional, and spiritual. So many young people are settling for the physical aspects only and are cheating themselves of the emotional and spiritual aspects of sex. Sadder still, is that sex improves dramatically as each level is achieved. Surprisingly, the physical is easy to achieve but offers the least in return. Bring the emotional component to a relationship the physical gets even better. And with total commitment, which we call marriage, the spiritual comes into play. It serves to raise the stakes even higher, for both the physical aspect and the emotional aspect. When all three are working in concourse, it is easy to see how many couples are able to enjoy a lifelong commitment to one another.

Final Thoughts

The issues of sex and sexuality are long standing. Some things have remained fairly constant over time and others have seen dramatic change. For what my opinion is worth, I think guys have remained pretty much the same over the past million years. They have always liked sex and they have always done pretty much everything in their power to get sex. Girls, on the other hand, have changed more dramatically. Time was, that girls were very choosy about who they ultimately decided to mate with. They used their brains. Something odd happened to some women at about the time of the sixties' liberation movement. While a lot of good might well have been accomplished, one disturbing trend evolved. Some women used the opportunity provided by the equal rights amendment, to become as equally stupid as some men.

Discernment went out the window and the trend has only worsened over the decades since the sixties. Do you know nearly every female animal on earth will choose not to mate with her male counterpart until he has proven himself? A pride of lions, for example, will originally consist of a near equal number of males and females. The males do all they can to mate with the females, but to no avail. The females will have nothing to do with the males and they are adamant about it! Eventually the males become rather frustrated by this inability to fulfill their reproductive destiny and they begin to fight among themselves. One by one the weaker of the males are driven off until just two remain. They will battle, often times for days, until one finally triumphs. The last of his competitors is forced into a solitary life. What happens next explains the serious nature of the battle between the males. Every female in the pride will now allow the male to mate with her. In fact, they even become sexually aggressive urging him to fulfill his reproductive destiny. There are times during the mating season, when the females will even band together and hunt so that they can supply food to the male. What caused the females to undergo such a dramatic change of attitude? The answer is rather simple. They waited until the male proved himself worthy. They want their cubs to have the best possible chances for survival. By mating with the biggest and baddest cat of all, they are endowing their offspring with qualities that will prove immensely valuable in their own survival.

Certain species of female penguin will simply not mate until the male can show them to a suitable nest for them and their future hatchlings. The stronger the male, the better the nest, which allows him to attract the more prized female. Female cockroaches even have standards. Males put on fancy displays of physical prowess in order to attract the females. Only the ones that pass muster will mate.

Lions, penguins, and even cockroaches, females of nearly every species make their male counterparts prove themselves before they will mate. One of the species that has forgone this qualification process is humans. Many females of this species will mate with little, if any, proof that the male will be able to provide for her and their offspring. The statistics bear that out, so many women and their children are left to fend for themselves. Women need to make much better use of their ability to discern. They also need to use patience in evaluating a suitable mate.

If girls only knew that they are the ones with all the power when it comes to this thing called sex. They can make a guy follow her to the ends of the earth in pursuit of her sexuality. Holding that dear, and thus holding it back, can be one of the greatest lures of all time. But once they give it up to a guy, 97-percent of the time he is on to the next challenge. Girls have a choice. They can be diamond or they can be dirt. Diamonds are valuable because they are rare and hard to get. Dirt is cheap because it is so readily available. Which would you rather your daughter be?

I guess it comes down to this. Why abstinence? Why not take a more 'comprehensive" approach? It is really quite simply. The pro-comprehensive lobby, (comprised of the likes of the condom industry, Planned Parenthood and certain pharmaceutical companies) loves to state that abstinence does not work. Well, common sense alone tells us what a deception this is. Of course abstinence works. If people do not engage in sexual activity, they won't risk a disease or a pregnancy. So, preaching abstinence is absolutely the best way to protect our next generations. Why not a 'comprehensive' approach? It is simple. That approach can put our young people in harm's way. That is unacceptable. In fact, I find the use of the word 'comprehensive' to be a deception in itself. Let's face it, 'permissive' is a much better choice of words. For the balance of this chapter, let's just call a spade a spade.

So why do certain elements push for the permissive agenda? In a word – money. For the manufacturers of condoms and birth control drugs like the pill and Norplant, the connection is a simple one. The more people are having sex, the more their products are needed. As for Planned Parenthood the connection is a little more circuituitous. While they certainly advise the use of birth control devices and drugs they actually make a killing when they fail. And I honestly don't mean that as a lousy pun. Worldwide, one of the biggest funding sources for Planned Parenthood is performing abortion. How many businesses can you think of that make even more money when their initial advice fails?

As for the abstinence movement, you may be surprised to know we receive absolutely no financial reward for having young people follow our advice. Our reward comes in the form of fewer broken dreams. Fewer unplanned pregnancies. Fewer STD infections.

Through it all, I caution you to think for yourself and do not accept things at face value. Even this book. There are ongoing arguments about the liberal vs. conservative bias in the media. In my opinion, bias is only a bad thing when it supports mythology. When bias is toward the truth, well that is just enthusiasm for what is right. The discernment is yours and yours alone. However, allow me by way of a quote to tell you where at least one reporter for the well-known Cleveland Plain Dealer stands. In a recent article, she expressed her utter dismay for the whole concept of abstinence only education. Allow me to quote one of her major concerns, directly from her article, "Abstinence only education is intrinsically moral". Would anyone like to write and tell me just what is so wrong about that?

Web Resources

The official website of our very own Marriage First Abstinence only education program.
                                         www.factsaboutsex.com

The Abstinence Clearinghouse serves as an association
for the abstinence community. The Clearinghouse is a nonprofit, educational organization that promotes the appre-
ciation for and the practice of, sexual abstinence through
distribution of age-appropriate, factual and medically accurate materials.   **www.abstinence.net**

The Center's for Disease Control and Prevention (CDC)
is one of the 13 major operating components of the Department of Health and Human Services (HHS), which is
the principal agency in the United States government for
protecting the health and safety of all Americans and for
providing essential human services, especially for those
who are least able to help themselves.   **www.cdc.gov**

Focus on the Family, founded by Dr. James Dobson was
established to cooperate with the Holy Spirit in dissemi-
nating the Gospel of Jesus Christ to as many people as
possible, and, specifically, to accomplish that objective by
helping to preserve traditional values and the institution
of the family.   **www.family.org**

Forever Families provides practical, scholarly and sacred information for strengthening individuals, marriages and families of all faiths, organized around themes of the family.

www.foreverfamilies.net

The Louisiana Governor's Program on Abstinence is a well-respected, statewide initiative to educate the citizens of Louisiana as to the benefits of abstinence until marriage. They offer a terrific and very informative weekly e-news-letter.   **www.abstinencedu.com**

The Medical Institute for Sexual Health is a nonprofit scientific, educational organization founded in 1992 by obstetrician/gynecologist, Joe S McIlhaney, Jr. MD to confront the global epidemics of non-marital pregnancy and sexually transmitted disease with incisive health care data.

www.medinstitute.org

Teen-Aid is a not-for-profit organization started in 1981 for the special purpose of reducing out-of-wedlock teen pregnancies and their many consequences. The method believed most valuable was abstinence education, which stresses character development and connection to parents.

www.teen-aid.org

Books Worth Reading

The following twelve books were valuable resources in the writing of this book. Between Jen and I, we have read all of the books listed below. They are rich with information and resources and are definitely worth reading.

The descriptions that follow each title are a combination of my thoughts and the actual words on the cover of each book.

ON SEX AND SEXUALITY:

SEX - What you don't know can kill you
By Joe S. McIlhaney Jr., M.D.

In a compassionate manner, trusted author and OB-GYN Joe McIlhaney helps singles develop a personal sexual code. This book describes in detail the powerful pitfalls of unchecked sexual activity. Dr. McIlhaney courageously explodes the myths of safe sex and exposes the truth of sexually transmitted diseases in today's "sexually enlightened" society.

Using current medical information, Dr. McIlhaney devotes entire chapters to STDs such as chlamydia, gonorrhea, herpes, HIV, and AIDS. In addition to the physical dangers of misusing sex, he discusses the emotional side effects. By following the doctor's guidelines, readers have little to fear.

SexSmart – 501 Reasons to Hold Off on Sex
By Susan Browning Progany

SexSmart is a thoughtful, pragmatic approach to a troubling subject. I applaud the sensitive dedication of Susan Browning Progany in helping teens understand the value of abstinence. This book is a must-read for teens and their parents.

This book is the indispensable guide to successful teenage love. This book tells it like it is, in plain talk that teens understand. Rich in common sense, facts, and anecdotes, *SexSmart* should be read by all teenagers and their parents. Sex educators in schools throughout this country would do well to include this book in their class work.

ON DATING:

Boundaries in Dating – Making Dating Work
By Dr. Henry Cloud & Dr. John Townsend

Between singleness and marriage lies the journey of dating. Want to make your road as smooth as possible? Set and maintain healthy boundaries – boundaries that will help you grow in freedom, honesty, and self-control.

If many of your dating experiences have been difficult, *Boundaries in Dating* could revolutionize the way you handle relationships. And even if you are doing well, the insights you'll gain from this much-needed book can help you fine-tune or even completely readjust important areas of your dating life.

Written by the authors of the best-selling book *Bound-aries*, *Boundaries in Dating* is your road map to the kind of enjoyable, rewarding dating that can take you from weekends alone to a lifetime with the soul mate of your dreams.

I Kissed Dating Goodbye
By Joshua Harris

Tired of the game? Kiss dating goodbye. Dating. Isn't there a better way? *I Kissed Dating Goodbye* suggests there is. Reorder your romantic life in the light of God's Word and find more fulfillment than a date could ever give – a life of sincere love, true purity and purposeful single-ness.

The 10 Commandments of Dating
By Ben Young & Dr. Samuel Adams

Are you tired of pouring time, energy, and money into relationships that start off great and end with heartache? Maybe you are frustrated because you cannot find "the one" for you, no matter how hard you pray, primp, and plead. If so, you need *The Ten Commandments of Dating* to give you the hard-hitting, black-and-white, practical guidelines that will address your questions and frustra-tions about dating. This guide will help you keep your head in the search for the desire of your heart. *The Ten Commandments of Dating* isn't more relationship advice. It's relationship common sense.

The Dating Trap
By Martha Ruppert

What dreams do you have for your children? What kind of marriage do you want your son or daughter to have? And what will it take to see those dreams come true? This book provides a wealth of information that will help to answer these questions.

Often young people end up in relationships that look far too much like those of the often times disastrous world around them. Poor dating patterns can lead to regrets and unhappy marriages. Is there a better way? Yes there is and it is explored fully in this book.

Martha Ruppert suggests practical alternatives to one-on-one dating relationships. It really does not matter whether your children are school aged, teenagers, or young adults, you can help them develop habits that will prepare them for healthy friendships, joyous courtship, and a satisfying marriage.

This book will help you help your children to be emotionally, spiritually, and socially healthy people who are equipped to avoid the very real dangers of the dating trap.

ON CHILDREN AND CHARACTER:

You're a Better Parent than you Think
By Raymond Guarendi, PhD.

Dr. Guarendi's approach to parenting is so replete with common sense and humor that you will not be able to put this book down. His writing style is comfortable and easy to read. His words offer reassurance to parents everywhere that they truly are doing a better job that they might realize.

The book is full of parenting tips that will take you beyond "good enough" and into "super-parent" status. Dr. Guarendi recognizes that children do not come with an instruction book so the job of parenting can seem a little daunting at times. This book is the instruction book parents are looking for!

Restoring the Teenage Soul
By Margaret J. Meeker, M.D.

As we enter the new millennium, the teenage years have never been more difficult. We can tell by their behavior: School shootings. Teen Pregnancy. Fatal car crashes. Binge drinking. Dropping out.

But now's not the time to give up on the next generation, says author Meg Meeker, a Michigan child and adolescent physician, who has worked closely with teens for twenty years. Teens, she believes, are crying out for help - and it is up to the parents and other adults in their lives to respond.

Restoring the Teenage Soul will help you understand why our teens are getting into trouble. Why teens are depressed and suicidal. Why teens are looking for love in the wrong places. Dr. Meeker contends that the fundamental needs of teens are not being met, which results in them trying to find their own way in an unfriendly culture. Yet all is not lost, if adults are willing to be there for the teens in their lives.

Uplifting, frank, encouraging and conversational, *Restoring the Teenage Soul* will inspire any adult to get involved.

Raising Sexually Pure Kids
By Tim & Beverly LaHaye

If you are like a lot of parents, you hesitate to give simple, honest answers to kids' questions about sex because you're afraid they're "not ready" or it's too embarrassing to discuss. But if you don't answer their questions, who will? Television? Teammates? Public school "health" classes? The fact is, they'll learn about it from someone, and then who knows what they'll hear.

In *Raising Sexually Pure Kids*, Tim and Beverly LaHaye explain:
- Exactly what to tell children at different ages
- What to tell girls about boys, and boys about girls
- How to present sex in and open, healthy manner
- How to encourage children who have given in to temptation

Right From Wrong – What You Need to Know to Help Youth Make Right Choices
By Josh McDowell & Bob Hostetler

The headlines scream daily of classroom violence, children selling drugs, gang killings, and rampant teenage sex – the natural behavior of a generation that has lost its belief in objective right and wrong. To them, truth is a matter of taste: morality of individual preference.

And these are not just the kids across the street; they are the young people in our own churches – in our own families. Church leaders and parents are painfully aware that their kids are veering away from values at an alarming rate. Josh McDowell's new, extensive study of churched youth shows that 57 percent cannot affirm that an objective standard for right and wrong even exists. This was just one troubling fact uncovered by McDowell.

In *Right from Wrong* Josh McDowell along with Bob Hostetler provide the tools to reverse this alarming decline. In vintage McDowell fashion, this book provides families and church with a "truth apologetic" – a defense of truth that will enable adults to equip their youth with the ability to resist the erosion of their values and determine what is right from wrong.

Right from Wrong offers not a quick fix, but a thorough, biblical and practical blueprint for understanding moral absolutes and passing on core values to the next generation.

Sex and Character
By Deborah Cole & Maureen Gallagher Duran

With *Sex and Character*, the authors and producers have made an enormous contribution to the children of America on behalf of all who care about their welfare. The destruction of our young is no narrow, sectarian concern. Whether black or white, Hispanic or Eastern, Republican or Democrat, liberal or conservative, we all want our children to grow up with sound guidance from the adults in their lives, guidance that will allow them to develop integrity and strong character. We want this for our youth because with the inner strength of sound values, they are less likely to engage in risky behaviors while they are young. As a result, they are more likely to enjoy physical and emotional health, first as young adults and later as mature adults.

As adults use this book, they will not only gain up-to-date insight on why good character is indispensable, but how to teach it. Young people will learn what good character is and that by becoming a person of strong character they can have lives more full of meaning, more free of difficulties, with greater hope for the future.

ON UNCOVERED DECEPTION:

Grand Illusions – The Legacy of Planned Parenthood
By George Grant

Thoroughly researched, carefully written, and comprehensively documented, Grand Illusions has already made its mark as the single best-selling volume of all time on Planned Parenthood's role in the controversial matters of abortion and sex education. No other book has so thoroughly surveyed the divisive issues, dominating personalities, legal and judicial precedents, educational and political initiatives, social consequences, and global impact of this organization and the great debates it has engendered worldwide.

Condom Nation – Blind Faith, Bad Science
By Richard A. Panzer

Think condoms are the answer to protecting your child? Think again.

The fact that an untested prevention strategy is being advocated does not bother them. Why should it? The Condom Nation is nothing if not slick. In a world of latex, content can be replaced by style, by "cool: Questions about content are covered over by packaging, by labels, like "abstinence-based," that mean the opposite of what is implied. Words that once had clear meanings are made to serve whatever purpose the reigning ideology of sexual "diversity" demands. Words that cannot be reengineered are banished and replaced by nice-sounding terms that obscure the original meanings.

Studies are said to support the exact opposite of what they conclude. Much of the public is lulled into a feeling of complacency by terms like "protected sex," assisted by a docile, cooperative mainstream media that often follows a "don't ask, don't tell" policy when it comes to proclamations of "fact." Parents and groups who question content are vilified, forever banished outside the great latex wall that surrounds government-approved arbiters of reality.

KINSEY: Crimes & Consequences
By Judith A. Reisman, PhD.

In 1948, the Institute for Sex Research at Indiana University was led by eugenicist Alfred C. Kinsey, whose sex research shook America's moral foundations and launched the 1960's Sexual Revolution. Fifty years later new revelations confirm Dr. Judith Reisman's 1981 expose of scientific fraud and criminally derived data contained in the publicly funded Kinsey Reports. Dr. Reisman revealed that Kinsey conducted human experiments in a soundproof laboratory built to his specifications at Indiana University, and that the sexual abuse of at least 317 infants and young boys was a scientific protocol for Kinsey's 1948 report. Dr. Reisman discloses for the first time the ongoing consequences to the American people and the world based on Kinsey's deliberately skewed research. Kinsey died in 1956 but his Institute endures today under the expanded title of "The Kinsey Institute for Research in Sex, Gender, and Reproduction." Suggesting an even more ominous threat to human rights and liberty.

Dr. Judith Reisman offers this very intense book in an effort to end the 50-year Kinsey era of "hush and pretend" which has been so devastating to women and children. Read and discover for the sake of your children and children everywhere

Contributors and Other Sources of Inspiration

The following list of contributors contains both voluntary and involuntary contributors.

Jennifer Werstler–my long time co-presenter, and keeper of the reams of student comments and questions that form the core of this book. Her youthful presence brought new life to a program that had tired under my solo effort. She stands as a living example that you can indeed, delay the onset of sexual activity and put marriage first.

Rhiannon, Abigail, Katie, Jennifer, Hallie, Audrey, Alysa, Brittany, Anastasia, Hope, Harmony, Faith, Lauren, Heather, Katy, Jessica, Angela, Kayleigh, Susan, Holly, Amy, Melanie, and Erica, are just some of the many teen girls who continue to prove to me that abstinence is not only achievable but desirable.

Hallie Kloots, age 15, and my teen issues consultant

Many thanks to the education professionals, who took a chance and invited us into their classroom, and kept inviting us back. Larry Taylor-Jackson High School, Tamiko Hatcher-Lehman Middle School, Theresa Lattanzi-Alliiance City Schools, Jim Rubin-Timken High School, Doug Miller-Central Catholic High School, Mike Ress-St. Michael, Mary Fiala-St. Joan of Arc, Dimitri Holston–Hartford Middle School, Debbie Lily-Central Catholic High School, Jason Werstler-Lorin Andrews Middle School, Natalie Morrison-Souers Middle School, Theresa Montgomery-Alliance Middle School, Anne Bradway-Hoover High School, Scott Akers-Jackson High School, Todd Krino-R.G.Drage, Kim Kuhns-Navarre Elementary, Tess Albaugh-St. Barbara, Sue Schmader-Our Lady of Peace, Fr. Robert Kaylor-Central Catholic High School, Anne Weeks-Holy Spirit, Debbie Capretta- Regina Coeli-St. Joseph Alliance, Kathy Harbert-McKinley High School.

To the hundreds of students who have shared their questions and thoughts via our classroom visits, our web site and our radio show. I am always impressed by the potential that I see in our young people.

To Brad and Heidi Sellers, friends of mine and parents of ten children. Half of those ten are now productive and contributing members of our community. The other half is still in the process of being raised. If the Sellers can manage such terrific results with their ten, then the rest of us should have little trouble with our 2.3 children.

An amazing array of editors including my daughters Abigail and Rhiannon, wife Wendy, coworkers Ruth, Tina, Amy, Jen, Kayleigh and former coworker Christine Nardis – for taking the time to apply her vast knowledge of Strunk and White to the above copy. Her English skills are second to none. Additionally, she has stood on the front lines with me and developed a character education program for the city of Alliance, Ohio.

Debra Martin, Scott Spencer, Todd Larson, Heather McKimm and Erica Katizback all local and all very outstanding abstinence education presenters.

Pam Stenzel, perhaps the top presenter in the entire field. I enjoyed chauffeuring Pam around my hometown as she spoke at a dozen assembly presentations in four days. Abstinence presenters all say about the same thing, after all, the truth is the truth. With Pam, her ceaseless passion makes her the best!

Mike Worley is, for my money, the best male presenter in the field of abstinence education, and is a real inspiration to other males in the field.

The National Abstinence Clearinghouse, under the leadership of Leslie Unruh, is the premier abstinence education organization in the world. You can check them out in the web site section.

And as with every book I write, thank you Lisa.

Bibliography

Alan Guttmacher Institute. *Sex and America's Teenagers.* New York, 1994.

Antonio, Gene. *AIDS: Rage and Reality.* Dallas: Anchor Books, 1992.

Calderone, Dr. Mary S., and Dr. James Ramey. *Talking with Your Child about Sex.* New York: Random House, 1982.

Cloud, Dr. Henry and Dr. John Townsend. *Boundaries in Dating.* Grand Rapids: Zondervan Publishing House, 2000.

Cole, Deborah D. and Maureen Gallagher Duran. *Sex and Character.* Dallas: Haughton Publishing Company, 1998.

Coles, Robert and Geoffrey Stokes. *Sex and the American Teenager.* New York: Harper & Row, 1985.

Comstock, George. *Television in America.* Beverly Hills: Sage Press, 1980.

"Condoms, Contraceptives, and Sexually Transmitted Disease." Research Triangle Park, N.C.: American Social Health Association, 1995.

Conley, Dalton. *The Pecking Order.* New York: Pantheon Books, 2004.

Connolly, Cecil. "Abstinence Moves to the Head of the Class." *Washington Post* (April 24, 2002): A3

Cook, Bruce. *The Big Talk Book.* Marietta, Georgia: Choosing the Best, LLC, 2002.

Fox, Roy F. *Harvesting Minds: How TV Commercials Control Kids.* Westport, Connecticut: Praeger, 1996.

Guarendi, Dr. Raymond. *You are a Better Parent than You Think.* New York: Simon & Schuster, 1992.

Gordon, Dr. Sol and Judith Gordon, M.S.W. *Raising a Child Conservatively in a Sexually Permissive World.* New York: Simon and Schuster, 1983.

"GPA Progress Report." Baton Rouge, Louisiana: The Louisiana Governor's Report on Abstinence, 2003.

Grant, George. *Grand Illusions, The Legacy of Planned Parenthood.* Nashville: Cumberland House, 2000.

Habib, Dan. "Teen Sexuality in a Culture of Confusion." Knox Turner Associates (1995).

Harris, Joshua. *I Kissed Dating Goodbye.* Sister, Oregon: Multnomah Books, 1997.

Kahn, Joan and Kathryn London, "Premarital Sex and the Risk of Divorce," *Journal of Marriage and Family,* November 1991, 845-55.

LaHaye, Beverly and Tim. *Raising Sexually Pure Kids.* Sisters, Oregon: Multnomah Books, 1998.

Lambert, James. *Porn in America.* Lafayette, Louisiana: Huntington House Publishers, 1997.

Marr, Dr. Lisa. *Sexually Transmitted Diseases.* Baltimore: Johns Hopkins University Press, 1998.

Marshall, Robert and Charles Donovan. *Blessed are the Barren.* San Francisco: Ignatius Press, 1991.

McDowell, Josh and Bob Hostetler. *Right From Wrong.* Dallas: Word Publishing, 1994.

McIlhaney, Dr. Joe Jr. *Sex What You Don't Know Can Kill You.* Grand Rapids: Baker Books, 1997.

Meeker, Dr. Margaret. *Restoring the Teenage Soul.* Traverse City, Michigan: McKinley and Mann, 1999

Mueller, Walt. *Understanding Today's Youth Culture.* Wheaton, Illinois: Tyndale House Publishers, 1999.

Mulrine, Anne. "Risky Business." *U.S. News and World Report* 132 (May 27, 2002): 42.

Panzer, Richard A. *Condom Nation Blind Faith Bad Science.* Westwood, N.J.: Center for Educational Media, 1997.

Pogany, Susan Browning. *SexSmart.* Minneapolis: Fairview Press, 1998.

Reisman, Dr. Judith A. *Kinsey: Crimes and Consequences.* Arlington, Virginia: Institute for Medical Education, Inc., 1998.

Ruppert, Martha. *The Dating Trap.* Chicago: Moody Press, 2000.

"SEER Cancer Statistics Review 1975-2000." National Cancer Institute (NCI).

Seligmann, Jean. "Condoms in the Classroom." *Newsweek* 118 (December 9, 1991): 61.

Sellers, Abbylin and Jerry Gzranckow. "Dashing to Decadence." Focus on the Family. 2001

Tannahill, Reay. *Sex in History.* Briar Cliff Manor, New York: Scarborough House Publishers, 1992.

"The Green Behind a Planned Parenthood "White Paper". A Made4More Public Policy Brief: Focus on the Family.

Westermarck, E. *History of Human Marriage.* London, 1891.

Whitehead, Barbara. "The Failure of Sex Education." *The Atlantic Monthly* (October, 1994).

Young, Ben and Dr. Samuel Adams. *The Ten Commandments of Dating.* Nashville: Thomas Nelson Publishers, 1999.

About the Author

Raymond Fete is the founder and director of the Marriage First abstinence only education program. The Marriage First program was developed locally but is nationally recognized and serves as the model for similar programs in 22 states. Ray has delivered his 'abstinence until marriage' message to more than 100,000 young people over the years. Marriage First has received nationwide press coverage and Ray has been quoted in Newsweek, USA Today, Time, The Wall Street Journal, and numerous other publications.

Ray is a life long native of Canton, Ohio and is a 1971 graduate of Massillon Perry High School and a 1975 graduate of Kent State University, where he majored in both psychology and geography. In addition to his duties as the director of Marriage First, Ray runs a family homeless shelter operated by Community Services of Stark County, Inc. He also serves as their Director of New Program and Fund Development. Ray is also the girls' basketball coach for St. Joseph School in Canton, Ohio, where he has served in that volunteer position for 23 years.

He makes his home outside of Massillon, Ohio with his wife Wendy. Together, they have three adult children and two grandchildren.